IMPERIUM ET CIVITAS

Excerpt from Trajan's column which was built in Emperor Trajan's honour after he conquered Dacia. Covered with carvings portraying the Dacian wars, the column was dedicated in A.D. 113. Today, the column, 38 m tall, stands in Trajan's Forum in Rome.

THEMES IN LATIN LITERATURE

amor et amicitia
imperium et civitas
multas per gentes
urbs antiqua

IMPERIUM ET CIVITAS

A COLLECTION OF LATIN PASSAGES SELECTED
FROM HISTORY, POETRY, SPEECHES, AND LETTERS
WITH VOCABULARY, NOTES, AND QUESTIONS

COMPILED AND EDITED BY PATRICIA E. BELL

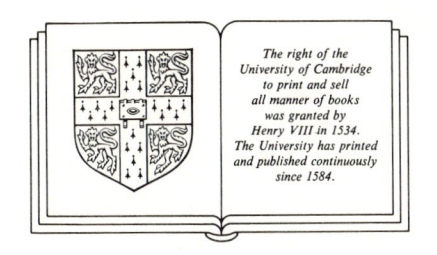

*The right of the
University of Cambridge
to print and sell
all manner of books
was granted by
Henry VIII in 1534.
The University has printed
and published continuously
since 1584.*

CAMBRIDGE UNIVERSITY PRESS
Cambridge
New York   Port Chester   Melbourne   Sydney

Published by the Press Syndicate of the University of Cambridge
The Pitt Building, Trumpington Street, Cambridge CB2 1RP
32 East 57th Street, New York, NY 10022, USA
10 Stamford Road, Oakleigh, Melbourne 3166, Australia

© Irwin Publishing Inc., Canada, 1988

First published 1988 by Irwin Publishing Inc., Canada

This edition first published 1989

Printed in Great Britain at the University Press, Cambridge

British Library cataloguing-in-publication data

Imperium et civitas: a collection of Latin
    passages selected from history, poetry, speeches,
    and letters with vocabulary, notes and questions.
    1. Latin language, – Readers
    I. Bell, Patricia E.
    478.6'421

Library of Congress cataloging-in-publication data

Imperium et civitas: a collection of latin passages selected from
    history, poetry, speeches, and letters with vocabulary, notes and
    questions/compiled and edited by Patricia E. Bell.
    Reprinted. Originally published: Richmond Hill, Ont.: Irwin Pub.,
    1988.
    Includes bibliographies.
    1. Latin language – Readers. I. Bell, Patricia E.
    PA2095.I47 1989
    478.6'421 – dc19   88-35169 CIP

ISBN 0 521 37737 4

Cover photograph: Excerpt from Trajan's column which was built in Emperor Trajan's honour after he conquered Dacia. Covered with carvings portraying the Dacian wars, the column was dedicated in A.D. 113. Today, the column, 38m tall, stands in Trajan's Forum in Rome.

Typeset by Jay Tee Graphics Ltd.

Table of Contents

Note to the Teacher VIII
To the Student IX
Glossary of Some Literary Terms Used in *Themes in Latin Literature* X
Short Biographies of Latin Authors Quoted in *imperium et civitas* XII

	No. of Lines	Page

THE THEORETICAL VIEW

Cicero Defines Statesmanship	18	2
Cicero, *Pro Sestio* 68		
Pliny Gives Advice to a New Governor	26	4
Pliny, *Epistulae* VIII.24		
Questions		6
Further Reading		6

THE PRACTICAL VIEW

Provincial Government		7
I The Conscientious Governor		8
The Need for Provincial Reform	14	8
Pliny, *Epistulae* X.32		
An Aqueduct in Nicomedia	20	10
Pliny, *Epistulae* X.37, 38		
A Sewer for Amastris	14	12
Pliny, *Epistulae* X.98, 99		
A Theatre and Gymnasium for Nicaea	31	14
Pliny, *Epistulae* X.39, 40		
Party Favours	16	16
Pliny, *Epistulae* X.116, 117		
II The Disreputable Governor		18
The Case Against Verres		18
The Significance of the Case	22	20
Cicero, *In Verrem* I.1.1-3; 16.46, 47		
The Charges Against Verres	24	22
Cicero, *In Verrem* I.4.12; 5.13-15		

	No. of Lines	Page
The Looting of Art Treasures	25	24
Cicero, *In Verrem* II.iv.1.1-2		
The Case of Heius' Chapel Ornaments	47	26
Cicero, *In Verrem* II.iv.2.3-8		
The Peroration	17	30
Cicero, *In Verrem* II.v.72.184, 186, 188-189		
Questions		32
Further Reading		34

THE PATRIOTIC VIEW

	No. of Lines	Page
In Praise of Roman Rule	34	36
Tacitus, *Histories* IV.73-74		
A Thanksgiving Ode	32	40
Horace, *Odes* I.37		
Regulus: A Model Roman	56	44
Horace, *Odes* III.5		
Questions		50
Further Reading		50

THE CRITICAL VIEW

	No. of Lines	Page
The Disastrous Years	20	52
Tacitus, *Histories* I.ii		
Calgacus' Speech	28	56
Tacitus, *Agricola* 29-30		
Questions		58
Further Reading		58

THE VISIONARY VIEW

	No. of Lines	Page
The Return of the Golden Age	33	60
Vergil, *Eclogues* IV.1-16, 37-52		
Rome's Mission	7	64
Vergil, *Aeneid* VI.847-853		
Questions		66
Further Reading		66

In memoriam: in loving memory of my husband, John M. Bell, who shared with me his love of learning and his love of teaching.

Note to the Teacher

This text is designed to provide you with readings suitable for students beginning to read original Latin. The Latin of all the selections is either unadapted or only very mildly edited. What editing there is takes the form of deletion rather than that of alteration.

Over 400 lines are offered here for an investigation of the theme of *imperium et civitas*. Additional readings for the further pursuit of each aspect of the theme are given at the end of each subtopic. A large part of *Aeneid* VI, central to any discussion of Roman nationalism, may be found in *multas per gentes*, a module in this same series, *Themes in Latin Literature*.

Since each selection is a self-contained unit with its own notes and vocabulary, there is no need to read every selection. Nor is it necessary to read the selections in the order given here.

The discussion questions at the end of each subtopic are intended to be directional, not comprehensive, and can readily be adapted to suit whatever selections you have chosen to read.

TO THE STUDENT

For convenience of discussion and comparison, the selections in this text have been organized according to subtopics of the theme of *imperium et civitas*. The letters, speeches, and poetry reveal Roman attitudes to imperialism and diplomacy, ranging from the practical to the visionary, from the patriotic to the vitriolic.

Notes and vocabulary have been included to assist you in your translating of each selection. Since sound and rhythm are important in both prose and poetry, you should read all selections aloud not only at the beginning of your study, but also at the conclusion of your analysis and discussion. In this way, you should be able to impart to your second reading all your new understanding of the passage.

The Initial Questions at the end of each section are intended to highlight only certain aspects of each passage. They should lead you into detailed analysis of the writer's treatment of the theme. They should not predetermine or limit your own exploration or the class discussion. You are expected to quote the Latin words and phrases that support your views and conclusions for every question.

The Discussion Questions are more general. They are designed to help you assess the distinctiveness of each writer's artistic conception of the theme, to form conclusions about the similarities and differences in approach of the different writers, and to explore and assess the effectiveness of the Roman expression of the theme.

Glossary of Some Literary Terms Used in *Themes in Latin Literature*

In writing a literary appreciation for a piece of literature, it is not enough simply to list literary devices and examples. Always examine critically each device to see how the writer uses it and what effect is achieved by its use in that context.

anaphora: the repetition of an important word at the beginning of several successive clauses

alliteration: the repetition of the same sound, usually a consonant, at the beginning of two or more adjacent words

antithesis: a rhetorical contrast achieved by the balanced or parallel arrangement of words, clauses, or sentences with a strong contrast in meaning

assonance: the repetition of the same vowel sounds in two or more adjacent words

asyndeton: the omission of conjunctions or customary connecting words

atmosphere: the mood pervading the literary work

cadence: a measured rhythmic sequence or flow of words in prose or poetry

connotation: the cluster of implicit or associated meanings of a word as distinguished from that word's denotative or specific meaning

diction: the deliberate choice of words

ellipsis: the omission of word(s) necessary for the grammatical structure of a sentence

emphatic word order:
- (i) **chiasmus**: a criss-cross arrangement usually resulting from the separation of two nouns and the adjectives that modify each
- (ii) **first and last word positions**: placing an important word at these emphatic positions in a line of poetry
- (iii) **framing**: a word placed out of its usual order and "framed" by a pair of related words to make the word stand out prominently
- (iv) **interlocking word order**: the words of one noun-adjective phrase alternating with those of another
- (v) **juxtaposition**: two words or phrases set side by side to intensify meaning
- (vi) **separation**: separating grammatically related words (e.g., noun—noun, noun—adjective) to produce a word picture of the meaning conveyed by the words

epic: a long narrative poem in elevated style, typically having as its subject a hero on whose exploits depends to some degree the fate of a nation or race

epic simile: a comparison extended beyond the obvious comparison by further details

epigram: a brief and pointed poem, usually ending with a surprising or witty turn of thought

figurative language: language that departs from the literal standard meaning in order to achieve a special effect, e.g., metaphor, personification, simile

genre: a literary form, e.g., epic, lyric, satire

hyperbole: an extravagant exaggeration of fact used to express strong feeling and not intended to be taken literally

imagery: the poetic technique of making mental pictures in such a way as to make the emotion or mood appeal vividly to the reader and to produce a clue to poetic intent
interjection: a sudden phrase or word that interrupts the grammatical progress of the sentence
irony: the use of words that convey a sense or attitude contrary to what is literally expressed; e.g., often ostensible praise or approval implies condemnation or contempt
metaphor: an indirect comparison whereby one thing is compared to another without the expressed indication of the point of similarity
mythological allusion: a brief reference to mythological details the writer assumes will be readily recognized by the reader instead of stating directly the myth or name of the person or thing
onomatopoeia or imitative harmony: the use of a word whose sound resembles the sound it describes
oxymoron: a rhetorical contrast achieved by putting together two contradictory terms
paradox: a statement that seems contradictory but that reveals a coherent truth
parallelism or balanced structure: the recurrence or repetition of a grammatical pattern
pathos: the creation of pity or sorrow in the reader
periodic sentence: a sentence designed to arouse interest and suspense by keeping the meaning unclear until the very end
personification: the description of an inanimate object or concept in terms of human qualities
rhetoric: the presentation of ideas in a persuasive manner, usually used for effectiveness in oratory or public speaking; for specific rhetoric devices, see anaphora, alliteration, etc.
rhetorical question: a question used for its persuasive effect and for which no answer is expected or for which the answer is self-evident; it is used to achieve rhetorical emphasis stronger than a direct statement
rhythm: the pattern of long and short syllables in each line of poetry
rhyme: the repetition of the same sound at the end of two or more words
satire: a literary form in which prevailing vices or follies are held up to humour and ridicule and evoke towards them attitudes of amusement, indignation, or contempt
simile: a stated comparison often indicated by a term such as *velut*, *similis*, or *qualis*. A simile extended to embellish, complete, or reinforce the narrative with a vivid picture, the details of which are not always relevant to the original point of comparison, is called an **epic simile.**
theme: the central or dominating idea of a literary work
tone: the attitude of the writer to the subject. The tone may be characterized, for example, as formal or informal, solemn or playful, satirical, serious, or ironic.
transferred epithet: the application of a significant modifier to a word other than the one to which it actually belongs
vivid particularization: a concrete or specified description, usually achieved by the use of proper nouns rich in connotations

Short Biographies of Latin Authors Quoted in *Imperium et Civitas*

Cicero: Orator, Statesman, Philosopher, Letter Writer (106 B.C.—43 B.C.)

Marcus Tullius Cicero was born in Arpinum, southeast of Rome, of a family of equestrian rank. He studied rhetoric and philosophy in Rome. Although a *novus homo*, he advanced politically, even to positions usually reserved for patricians, because of his success as a lawyer. He was particularly respected because of his prosecution of Verres in 70 B.C. when he defeated the leading orator of the day, Quintus Hortensius. About 79 B.C., he married Terentia. He was acclaimed *pater patriae* in 63 B.C., when as consul he discovered and frustrated a revolutionary conspiracy led by Lucius Sergius Catilina. About 59 B.C., it appears that Gaius Julius Caesar attempted to win Cicero's approval for the newly formed (First) Triumvirate. However, Cicero refused to condone the unconstitutional nature of that governing group. Almost immediately the government passed a bill sending into exile anyone who had executed Romans without allowing an appeal. This bill was directed against Cicero who, as consul, had had the Catilinarian conspirators executed. A bitterly disillusioned Cicero left Italy in 58 B.C., but he was pardoned and recalled in 57 B.C. In 51 B.C., he was sent as governor to the province of Cilicia in Asia Minor. He returned to Italy to discover that Julius Caesar and Gnaeus Pompeius Magnus (Pompey the Great) had quarrelled, dissolving the First Triumvirate, and that civil war was imminent. After a period of confusion, Cicero made the agonizing decision to support Pompey. Although Pompey was defeated by Caesar, Caesar pardoned Cicero in 47 B.C. In 46 B.C., Cicero divorced his wife Terentia. The following year, his beloved daughter died. After the assassination of Caesar in 44 B.C., Cicero, hoping for a restoration of the old traditional republican order, began to denounce Marcus Antonius as the man who had tried to make Caesar a king. Unfortunately for Cicero, the Second Triumvirate was formed by Antony and Octavian (Caesar's heir and later known as Augustus), and Lepidus. With Octavian's reluctant consent, Cicero's name was put on the proscription list. Cicero was murdered by Antony's soldiers in 43 B.C.

Politically, Cicero was a moderate opposed to revolution and change. He was bewildered and confused by the political unrest in which he lived and he found it difficult to be decisive or consistent in the political dilemmas that faced him. However, his strengths in oratory, political theory, philosophy, and literary criticism made an incomparable impression on his own time and on subsequent European thought and literary style. Over 300 of his letters to family and friends survive, giving us an invaluable picture of both the man and this turbulent period of Roman history.

Horace: Poet (65 B.C.—8 B.C.)

Quintus Horatius Flaccus, born in Venusia in southern Italy, was the son of a freedman who contrived to give Horace the best education attainable both in Rome and in Athens. Horace served for some years as a clerk in the civil service in Rome while he wrote poetry. About 38 B.C., Horace was introduced by the poet Vergil to Maecenas who became Horace's patron. Maecenas in turn introduced Horace to the emperor Augustus and gave to Horace the Sabine Farm outside Rome which became Horace's beloved refuge from Rome. In 17 B.C., Horace was asked to write an official hymn celebrating ten years of peace under Augustus. In this way, Horace was openly recognized as the foremost lyric poet of Rome.

Horace's reputation lies mainly in his *Odes*, in which he adapted the traditional Greek lyric metres to the Latin language. The first three books of the *Odes* were composed between 33 B.C. and 23 B.C. The final book appeared about 15 B.C. Horace's poetry is characterized by unsurpassed technical mastery of language and metre. His polished verses with compressed and allusive use of language are the result of painstaking effort. His poems reveal a simple, sincere, friendly man of many interests. He is patriotic, good humoured, and tolerant. Horace is not the passionate participant in life but the amused onlooker.

Pliny the Younger: Letter Writer, Statesman (c. A.D. 61—c. A.D. 112)

Gaius Plinius Caecilius Secundus was born of the artistocracy of Comum, a lakeside town in northern Italy. He was adopted by his uncle, Pliny the Elder. At Rome, Pliny studied law, oratory, and philosophy. He rose steadily up the *cursus honorum* (the regular steps of the political ladder), becoming consul in A.D. 100 and then curator of the Tiber and its banks. About A.D. 110, he was sent, by special appointment by the emperor Trajan, to govern the Roman province of Bithynia in Asia Minor. He was to investigate and settle the unrest there. Pliny was married three times. His third marriage, to Calpurnia, was a very happy one.

Although he was a distinguished lawyer, only one of Pliny's speeches survives. However, over 200 of his letters survive and with them a vast quantity of useful information about the way of life during the first century A.D. His correspondence with Trajan provides a valuable picture of the administration of an imperial province. His style is characterized by his brevity, simplicity, and frankness as well as by a touch of a self-consciously literary style.

Tacitus: Historian (c. A.D. 56—c. A.D. 117)

Publius Cornelius Tacitus was probably born in one of Rome's Gallic provinces of a ranking Roman family. He appears to have studied rhetoric in Rome and then served in public office during the reigns of Vespasian, Titus, and Domitian. In A.D. 78, he married the daughter of Gnaeus Julius Agricola, who later became famous as the governor of Britian. Tacitus was in Rome in the early 90s during Domitian's reign of terror. Under emperor Trajan, he began to publish his historical works. The *Histories* dealt with the emperors from Galba to Domitian. The *Annals* covered the earlier Roman period from Tiberius to Nero.

Tacitus' historical writings reveal an acute insight into character and events. His style is vivid and dramatic, but his tone is subjective. By making use of the techniques he received from his rhetorical education, he influences the reader with his relentless pessimism and his emphasis on the oppressiveness of the early imperial system.

Vergil: Poet (70 B.C.—19 B.C.)

Publius Vergilius Maro was born near Mantua in northern Italy. He studied philosophy and rhetoric at Rome where he later enjoyed the patronage of Maecenas.

Maecenas introduced Vergil to the emperor Augustus. Vergil lived most of the time in Campania, a district around the Bay of Naples, where he had been given property by Augustus. About 43 B.C., Vergil began his earliest work, the *Eclogues*, a collection of pastoral poems. He spent the last eleven years of his life composing his chief work, the *Aeneid*. (The *Aeneid* is an epic, a long narrative poem, about Aeneas, a Trojan prince, who, after the fall of Troy, overcomes dangers and temptations to come at last to Italy and establish his followers there. Aeneas' descendants, the Julian family—including Augustus—would rule Rome and the world.) Vergil was modest about his poetic abilities and asked on his deathbed that the *Aeneid* be burned because it had not the polish and finish he desired. Augustus overruled his wishes and the poem was published.

Vergil was famous in his own time mainly as the epic poet who promoted a national pride in the Roman spirit and a sense of the glory of Rome's mission in the world. Vergil's poetry is characterized by the technical perfection of his metre, his sympathy with his characters, and the range and richness of his sound, imagery, and use of language.

THE THEORETICAL VIEW

Statue of Augustus from Prima Porta. Augustus, depicted here as *imperator*, was heralded as the guardian of the ancient traditions and the promoter of Rome's glorious destiny. (Rome, Vatican Museum)

Cicero Defines Statesmanship

imitemur nostros Brutos, Camillos, Decios, Curios, Fabricios, Scipiones, Lentulos, Aemilios, innumerabiles alios, qui hanc rem publicam stabiliverunt: quos equidem in deorum immortalium coetu ac numero repono. amemus patriam, pareamus senatui, consulamus bonis; praesentis fructus neglegamus, posteritatis gloriae serviamus; id esse optimum putemus, quod erit rectissimum; speremus quae volumus sed quod acciderit feramus; cogitemus denique corpus virorum fortium magnorumque hominum esse mortale, animi vero motus et virtutis gloriam sempiternam; neque, hanc opinionem si in illo sanctissimo Hercule consecratam videmus, cuius corpore ambusto vitam eius et virtutem immortalitas excepisse dicatur, minus existimemus eos, qui hanc tantam rem publicam suis consiliis aut laboribus aut auxerint aut defenderint aut servarint, esse immortalem gloriam consecutos.

CICERO, *PRO SESTIO* 68

Cicero Defines Statesmanship

This passage is taken from Cicero's defence in 56 B.C. of his friend Publius Sestius who was charged with creating public disorder. In this selection, Cicero delivers a political dissertation on the nature of the duties of a good citizen and statesman towards the state.

---

imitemur: hortatory subjunctive let us imitate
imitor, ari imitate
Brutos, Camillos, etc. plurals indicating types worthy of emulation
Brutus Lucius Iunius Brutus who freed Rome from its kings
Camillus Marcus Furius Camillus who freed Rome from the Gauls
Decii father and son, both consuls, both voluntarily died to save their country during wars in the early Republican era
Curius Marius Curius Dentatus who successfully led the Romans in several wars in the third century B.C. and who was noted for his moderate and restrained lifestyle
Fabricius Gaius Fabricius Luscinus who led the Roman army in the third century B.C. and was noted for his honesty and nobility towards the enemy
Scipiones Publius Cornelius Scipio Africanus Major and Publius Cornelius Scipio Aemilianus Africanus Minor who defeated the Carthaginians in the second and third Punic Wars respectively
Lentulus Publius Lentulus Spinther who was a friend of Cicero and had proposed the recall of Cicero from exile
Aemilius M. Aemilius Scaurus who was the chief justice of the court during the trial of Sestius

stabilio, ire, ivi establish, make stable
equidem indeed
coetus, us, m assembly, meeting
repono, ere place, count, reckon
amemus, pareamus, consulamus, etc.: hortatory subjunctives let us love, let us obey, etc.
consulo, ere + dat. have regard for
praesens, entis present
fructus, us, m enjoyment
neglego, ere disregard
posteritas, tatis, f posterity
servio, ire + dat. be subject to, serve
puto, are consider
rectus, a, um honest, upright
fero, ferre endure
vero truly
animi motus, us, m: motus is acc. pl. subject of inf. mental activity
sempiternus, a, um eternal
opinio, onis, f belief (i.e., in the immortality of *virtus*)
ambustus, a, um scorched
excipio, ere, cepi rescue
existimo, are consider, judge
consilium, i, n plan, deliberation
augeo, ere, auxi increase, enrich
servarint = servaverint
servo, are, avi guard, protect, keep safe
consequor, i, secutus reach, obtain

Pliny Gives Advice to a New Governor

C. PLINIUS MAXIMO SUO S.

cogita te missum in provinciam Achaiam, illam veram et meram Graeciam, in qua primum humanitas et litterae etiam fruges inventae esse creduntur; missum ad ordinandum statum liberarum civitatum.

reverere conditores deos et nomina deorum. reverere gloriam veterem et hanc ipsam senectutem, quae in homine venerabilis, in urbibus sacra. sit apud te honor antiquitati, sit ingentibus factis, sit fabulis quoque. nihil ex cuiusquam dignitate, nihil ex libertate, nihil etiam ex iactatione decerpseris. habe ante oculos hanc esse terram, quae nobis miserit iura, quae leges non victis sed petentibus dedit.

recordare quid quaeque civitas fuerit, non ut despicias quod esse desierit. absit superbia asperitas. nec timueris contemptum. an contemnitur qui imperium qui fasces habet, nisi humilis et sordidus, et qui se primus ipse contemnit? male vim suam potestas aliorum contumeliis experitur, male terrore veneratio adquiritur, longeque valentior amor ad obtinendum quod velis quam timor. nam timor abit si recedas, manet amor, ac sicut ille in odium hic in reverentiam vertitur.

quid ordinatione civilius, quid libertate pretiosius? porro quam turpe, si ordinatio eversione, libertas servitute mutetur!

PLINY, EPISTULAE VIII.24

Pliny Gives Advice to a New Governor

Pliny gives advice to his friend Maximus as Maximus sets out to govern Achaia, the Roman name for the province that comprised most of Greece.

C. = *Gaius*
S. = *salutem dat* sends greetings
cogito, are recognize, remember
missum = *missum esse*
merus, a, um genuine, pure, undiluted
humanitas, tatis, f humanity, civilization, culture
fruges, um, f agriculture
invenio, ire, veni, ventus find, discover
5 *ordino, are* set in order
status, us, m government, condition
civitas, tatis, f state, city-state
civitates liberae: normally, exempt from the governor's authority; Maximus went as a "corrector," a special legate appointed by the Emperor
revereor, vereri respect, revere
conditor, oris, m founder
vetus, veteris ancient
senectus, tutis, f age
venerabilis, e venerable
antiquitas, tatis, f antiquity
11 *iactatio, onis, f* pride, boasting
decerpo, ere, cerpsi take away
ius, iuris, n justice, law
lex, legis, f law
recordare: imperative of recordor, ari remember
desino, ere, desii cease

15 *superbus, a, um* haughty, proud
asperitas, atis, f harshness
contemptum = *contemptum esse*
an: *in a direct question where only one alternative is expressed* or then?
contemno, ere, tempsi, temptus scorn, despise
fasces, um, m fasces (bundle of wooden rods around an axe, insignia of power)
humilis, e mean
sordidus, a, um shabby, base, vile
vis, acc. vim, f strength, power
potestas, atis, f power, authority
contumelia, ae, f insult
experior, periri test
20 *veneratio, onis, f* respect
adquiro, ere acquire, get
valens, entis strong, powerful
recedo, ere go away, retire
sicut just as
ille...hic the former...the latter
verto, ere turn, change
ordinatione, libertate: abl. of comparison than order, than liberty
ordinatio, onis, f order
civilius: comparative degree more civilizing
25 *porro* furthermore
turpis, e disgraceful, shameful
eversio, onis, f an overturning
muto, are change

THEORETICAL VIEW

Initial Questions

Cicero Defines Statesmanship
1. Analyze this passage carefully and decide what Cicero thinks are the qualities of a good statesman.
2. What oratorical devices does Cicero use to persuade his listeners to his point of view?

Pliny Gives Advice to a New Governor
1. What makes this selection sound like instructions from a teacher? What effect might this approach have on the recipient of the letter? What does this selection suggest about the relationship of Pliny and Maximus?
2. Analyze this selection carefully and summarize Pliny's advice. Which pieces of advice seem sensible or practical? Which might be hard to apply in practice?

Discussion Questions

1. Compare Cicero's advice with that of Pliny. What points do both writers raise? Are there any points on which they disagree? Which selection is more practical? Can you suggest a reason for the difference between the two selections? Which passage is calculated to be more stirring? How does the writer achieve that effect?

Further Reading

Cicero gives advice to Curio: Cicero, *ad Familiares* 2.1.2
Cicero advises Mark Antony that to be the most powerful and so the most feared is not the true way to glory: Cicero, *Philippics* I.14.

THE PRACTICAL VIEW

Provincial Government

In the early years of Rome as a city-state, government office-holders were not paid any salary. Public service was expected of the patrician-senatorial families. As the city-state expanded into a world empire, the administration of the provinces fell to the same families who had already spent years campaigning for political office and holding public office at their own expense.

The governor of a province had absolute power during his year of service. Free from the control of Rome, he exercised complete control of all military, judicial, and administrative functions. He could not be removed from office nor prosecuted for government mismanagement during his term.

By the time of Cicero, these factors made possible the abuse of power by provincial governors. A governor might serve honestly, efficiently, and conscientiously. Pliny, who was governor of Bithynia many years after Cicero in A.D. 111, is a good example of an honest and responsible governor. But many governors tried to make enough money during their term of office to recoup their financial losses, pay off debts, and provide for the future. As a result, many provinces suffered from mismanagement and dishonesty. Verres who governed Sicily in 73-70 B.C. provides a good example of a corrupt governor and the effects that an unscrupulous ruler could have on a province.

I The Conscientious Governor

THE NEED FOR PROVINCIAL REFORM

TRAIANUS PLINIO

meminerimus idcirco te in istam provinciam missum, quoniam multa in ea emendanda adparuerint. erit autem vel hoc maxime corrigendum: quod qui damnati erant, non modo ea sine auctore, ut scribis, liberati sunt, sed etiam in condicionem proborum ministrorum retrahuntur. 5

  qui igitur intra hos proximos decem annos damnati nec ullo idoneo auctore liberati sunt, hos oportebit poenae suae reddi. si qui vetustiores invenientur et senes ante annos decem damnati, distribuamus illos in ea ministeria, quae non longe a poena sint. solent enim eiusmodi homines ad balineum, ad purgationes cloacarum, item munitiones viarum et vicorum dari. 10

PLINY, EPISTULAE X.32

The Need for Provincial Reform

In A.D. 111, Trajan, Emperor of Rome, sent Pliny on a special commission to Bithynia, a Roman province situated in modern Turkey. The province was besieged by political and financial problems. Pliny was to tour the province, maintain peace, remove irregularities and corruption in administration, and write reports. In one town, Pliny reports that convicted criminals, instead of being sent to the mines as sentenced, are working and drawing pay as public slaves. This is Trajan's reply to Pliny's report.

---

meminerimus: subjunctive let us remember
idcirco...quoniam for the very reason that
missum = missum esse
emendo, are correct, improve
adpareo or appareo, ere, ui appear, be manifest, be clear
vel...maxime especially
hoc: referring to the problem detailed in Pliny's letter and picked up in *quod*
corrigo, ere put straight, set right
quod the fact that
damno, are condemn, sentence
5 *non modo...sed etiam* not only...but also
auctor, oris, m authority
condicio, onis, f status
probus, a, um honest
minister, tri, m attendant
retraho, ere restore, take back
intra + acc. within

proximus, a, um last, most recent
idoneus, a, um proper
10 *poena, ae, f* punishment, penal servitude
si qui if any
vetustus, a, um old
distribuo, ere allocate
ministerium, i, n job: the cities saved money by having such jobs done by convicts rather than slaves
non longe a poena not too different from penal servitude
balineum, i, n public baths
purgatio, onis, f cleaning
cloaca, ae, f drain, sewer
item also, likewise
munitio, onis, f building, repairing
vicus, i, m street
do, are assign

An Aqueduct in Nicomedia

I C. PLINIUS TRAIANO IMPERATORI

in aquae ductum, domine, Nicomedenses impenderunt
HS |XXX| CCCXVIII. hic imperfectus adhuc omissus
et destructus etiam est. rursus in alium ductum erogata
sunt $\overline{CC}$. hoc quoque relicto, opus est novo impendio,   5
ut aquam habeant, qui tantam pecuniam male
perdiderunt.

necessarium est mitti a te vel aquilegem vel architectum, ne rursus eveniat quod accidit. ego illud unum
adfirmo, et utilitatem operis et pulchritudinem saeculo   10
tuo esse dignissimam.

PLINY, EPISTULAE X.37

II TRAIANUS PLINIO

curandum est, ut aqua in Nicomedensem civitatem
perducatur. vere credo te diligentia hoc opus
adgressurum. sed medius fidius ad eandem diligentiam
tuam pertinet inquirere, quorum vitio ad hoc tempus   5
tantam pecuniam Nicomedenses perdiderint, ne, dum
inter se gratificantur, et incohaverint aquae ductus et
reliquerint. quid itaque compereris, perfer in notitiam
meam.

PLINY, EPISTULAE X.38

An Aqueduct in Nicomedia

I The practical problems of water supply and drainage were of great interest to Pliny. He had exercised his expertise during his appointment to the Water and Drainage Board of the Tiber River Commission in Rome between A.D. 104 and A.D. 107. In this letter, Pliny reports that Nicomedia has spent vast sums of money on two aqueducts, each of which now lies abandoned and incomplete.

C. = Gaius
aquae ductus, us, m aqueduct
Nicomedenses the people of Nicomedia
impendo, ere, pendi expend, spend
HS |XXX| CCCXVIII 3 318 000 sesterces
imperfectus, a, um incompleted
omitto, ere, misi, missus abandon
destruo, ere, struxi, structus destroy, demolish
erogo, are, avi, atus pay out (i.e., especially money from public funds)
5 CC 200 000 sesterces

opus, eris, n need
impendium, i, n expenditure, outlay
perdo, ere, didi waste, squander
vel...vel either...or
aquilex, legis, m water engineer
evenio, ire turn out, happen, result
10 *adfirmo, are* assert
utilitas, tatis, f usefulness
opus, operis, n work
saeculum, i, n reign
dignus, a, um + abl. worthy of

II Trajan's reply acknowledges the need for an adequate water supply, but reminds Pliny of an equally urgent task.

---

curo, are to take care, pay attention to, take trouble to
civitas, tatis, f state, town, townspeople
perduco, ere lead, bring: especially of aqueducts
diligentia: abl. of manner with care, with diligence
adgressurum = adgressurum esse
adgredior, i, gressus sum approach, attack
medius fidius = me deus Fidius by the god of truth! good heavens!: Fidius was one name for Jupiter

5 *pertineo, ere + ad* fall upon, extend to
inquiro, ere investigate, find out
vitium, i, n fault
inter se gratificantur they are making a profit
incoho, are, avi begin
comperio, ire, peri find out, discover
perfero, ferre bring
notitia, ae, f notice, attention

A Sewer for Amastris

I C. PLINIUS TRAIANO IMPERATORI

Amastrianorum civitas, domine, et elegans et ornata habet inter praecipua opera pulcherrimam longissimamque plateam. cuius a latere porrigitur flumen, re vera cloaca foedissima, turpis immun- 5
dissimo adspectu et pestilens odore taeterrimo. quibus ex causis non minus salubritatis quam decoris interest eam contegi. quod fiet si permiseris curantibus nobis.

> PLINY, *EPISTULAE* X.98

II TRAIANUS PLINIO

rationis est, mi Secunde carissime, contegi aquam istam, quae per civitatem Amastrianorum fluit, si intecta salubritati obest. ne pecunia huic operi desit, curaturum te secundum diligentiam tuam certum 5
habeo.

> PLINY, *EPISTULAE* X.99

A Sewer for Amastris

I In the interests of hygiene and aesthetics, Pliny asks for authority to cover an open sewer in the city of Amastris. Imperial permission was necessary for any new construction.

C. = Gaius
civitas, tatis, f state, city, city-state
ornatus, a, um decorated, embellished
praecipuus, a, um extraordinary, special
platea, ae, f street
cuius a latere along its side
porrigo, ere stretch out, extend
5 *flumen, minis, n* stream
re vera in truth, really, actually
cloaca, ae, f sewer
foedus, a, um foul, filthy
turpis, e ugly, unsightly

immundus, a, um unclean, impure, foul
adspectus, us, m aspect, appearance
pestilens, entis noxious, unhealthy
odor, oris, m odour
taeter, tra, trum hideous, offensive
non minus...quam no less...than
salubritas, tatis, f health
decor, oris, m comeliness, beauty
interest + gen. it is of importance for
contego, ere cover
fio, fieri: used as passive of facio to be done
permitto, ere, misi + dat. entrust
curo, are take care of it

II Very few of Pliny's letters to Trajan from Bithynia seek advice on financial matters, on which Pliny was a recognized expert. In this reply, Trajan agrees that the unhealthy situation in Amastris needs attention and acknowledges Pliny's ability to handle the financial side of the project on his own initiative.

---

ratio, onis, f reason
intectus, a, um uncovered
obsum, esse + dat. be a danger to
desum, esse am lacking

5 *curaturum = curaturum esse*
secundum + acc. following, according to, in accordance with
certum habeo, ere know, am sure

A Theatre and Gymnasium for Nicaea

I C. PLINIUS TRAIANO IMPERATORI

theatrum, domine, Nicaeae maxima iam arte constructum, imperfectum tamen, sestertium amplius centies hausit; vereor ne frustra. ingentibus enim rimis desedit et hiat, sive solum umidum et molle, sive lapis ipse 5
gracilis et putris. dignum est certe deliberatione, sitne faciendum an sit relinquendum an etiam destruendum. nam fulturae ac substructiones non tam firmae mihi quam sumptuosae videntur. huic theatro ex privatorum pollicitationibus multa debentur, ut 10
basilicae circa, ut porticus supra caveam.

   idem Nicaeenses gymnasium incendio amissum ante adventum meum restituere coeperunt. architectus adfirmat parietes imposita onera sustinere non posse. cogor petere ut mittas architectum dispecturum utrum 15
sit utilius, post sumptum qui factus est, consummare opera, an quae videntur emendanda corrigere, an quae transferenda transferre.

PLINY, *EPISTULAE* X.39

II TRAIANUS PLINIO

quid oporteat fieri circa theatrum, quod incohatum apud Nicaeenses est, in re praesenti optime deliberabis et constitues. cum theatrum factum erit, tunc a privatis exige opera quae promissa sunt. 5

   gymnasiis indulgent Graeculi; ideo forsitan Nicaeenses maiore animo constructionem eius adgressi sunt. sed oportet illos eo contentos esse, quod possit illis sufficere.

   architecti tibi deesse non possunt. nulla provincia 10
non et peritos et ingeniosos homines habet. modo ne existimes brevius esse ab urbe mitti, cum ex Graecia etiam ad nos venire soliti sint.

PLINY, *EPISTULAE* X.40

A Theatre and Gymnasium for Nicaea

I Nicaea has spent a considerable sum of money on a theatre and a gymnasium, apparently without having the sites surveyed properly or the building materials inspected.

C. = Gaius
imperfectus, a, um incomplete
sestertium amplius centies more than ten million sesterces
haurio, haurire, hausi absorb, waste
rima, ae, f crack
desido, ere, sedi sink down, settle
5 *hio, are* gape, stand open
sive...sive whether...or
solum, i, n soil, ground
umidus, a, um wet
mollis, e soft
lapis, idis, m stone
gracilis, e thin
putris, tre rotten, crumbling
dignus, a, um + abl. worthy of
fultura, ae, f support, prop
substructio, ionis, f foundation
sumptuosus, a, um expensive, costly

9 *ex privatorum pollicitationibus multa (opera)* many additions promised by private individuals
ut such as
basilica, ae, f: a double colonnaded hall used as a meeting place and courthouse
supra + acc. above
gymnasium: a complex of changing and exercise rooms, lecture halls, and porticoes around an open exercise area
restituo, ere restore, rebuild
coepi have begun
adfirmo, are assert
paries, ietis, m wall
onus, eris, n weight
15 *dispicio, ere, spexi, spectus* decide
sumptus, us, m cost, expense
consummo, are complete
corrigo, ere set right, correct
transfero, ferre change

II Trajan replies with a hint of impatience.

---

incoho, are begin
in re praesenti being on the spot
delibero, are consider, weigh carefully
constituo, ere make a decision
5 *exigo, ere* exact, demand
indulgeo, ere + dat. revel in
Graeculi: a diminutive poor little Greeks: "Greek" and "Greece" were often used in a wider sense for a foreigner or foreign land
forsitan perhaps

maiore animo with too much ambition
adgredior, adgredi, adgressus sum undertake
sufficio, ere am adequate
desum, deesse + dat. lack
10 *architecti tibi deesse non possunt*: perhaps Trajan misses Pliny's point that the local architects may be in collusion with the city officials
ingeniosus, a, um clever, talented
modo only
ne existimes = noli existimare
ab urbe from Rome

PARTY FAVOURS

I C. PLINIUS TRAIANO IMPERATORI

qui virilem togam sumunt vel nuptias faciunt vel ineunt magistratum vel opus publicum dedicant, solent totam bulen atque etiam numerum e plebe vocare binosque denarios vel singulos dare. rogo scribas an 5 hoc celebrandum et quatenus putes. ipse enim arbitror, praesertim ex sollemnibus causis, concedendum ius invitationis. vereor tamen ne ii, qui mille homines etiam plures vocant, modum excedere et in speciem *dianomes* incidere videantur. 10

        PLINY, *EPISTULAE* X.116

II TRAIANUS PLINIO

merito vereris, ne invitatio in speciem *dianomes* incidat et in numero modum excedat. sed ego ideo prudentiam tuam elegi, ut formandis istius provinciae moribus ipse moderareris et ea constitueres, quae ad perpetuam 5 eius provinciae quietem essent profutura.

        PLINY, *EPISTULAE* X.117

Party Favours

I Pliny is concerned about the practice of inviting excessive numbers of public officials to private celebrations.

C. = Gaius
virilis toga the toga of manhood: the toga put on by Roman young men of fifteen or sixteen
sumo, ere put on
vel or
nuptiae, arum, f. pl. marriage
magistratus, us, m office
bule, es, f; bulen = acc. the (Greek) council
5 *binos denarios vel singulos* one or two *denarii*

quatenus how far, to what extent
sollemnis, e festive, ceremonial
concedo, ere allow, permit
ius, iuris, n the right
invitatio, onis, f reception
modus, i, m moderation, limit
excedo, ere go beyond, exceed
10 *species, ei, f* appearance, category
dianomes—a Greek word in gen. Tr. "of corrupt distribution of money"
incido, ere fall (into)

II Here, as elsewhere, Trajan reminds Pliny that his mission is to carry out the imperial policy of Trajan.

---

ideo for that very reason
eligo, ere, legi choose, select
formo, are shape, fashion, regulate
mores, ium, m. pl. conduct, character, morals
5 *moderor, ari + dat.* regulate, control, direct, govern
constituo, ere decide
prosum, prodesse, profui am useful, benefit, do good

II The Disreputable Governor

THE CASE AGAINST VERRES

Sent to Sicily as propraetor or governor in 73 B.C., Gaius Verres' one year service was extended to three because of an emergency in Rome. During his term, he abused his powers as governor to amass a large personal fortune. In 70 B.C., as soon as Verres left office and could be prosecuted, the Sicilian people approached Cicero to act for them. Cicero had been the quaestor or financial officer in Sicily in 75 B.C. and had earned a reputation for honesty and fairness. Although he was usually a defence lawyer, Cicero undertook the case, pitting himself against Verres' more experienced lawyer, Quintus Hortensius, recognized as Rome's leading legal orator.

The case came before a senatorial court composed, for the most part, of ex-governors or prospective governors. Cicero, with justification, claimed that Rome was watching to see if the senatorial judges would convict one from their own ranks. On the surface a case of extortion, the case, in fact, was an accusation of provincial mismanagement.

First Verres' defence tried to establish a friend as chief prosecutor. Cicero won the court case held to decide between the two claimants for prosecutor. Then, Cicero was allowed 110 days to collect evidence. The defence hoped to delay the hearings until the following year when the case would appear before judges more friendly to Verres. But within 50 days, Cicero had toured Sicily and returned to Rome. He had his case prepared so long before his opponents expected that he was able to secure court time for the current year. The final tactic left to the defence was to spin out the speeches and delay the conclusion of the case until the next year when the law would require a new trial before the new court.

The usual procedure of a First Hearing, the *actio prima*, was for the court to spend several days hearing lengthy formal speeches from the lawyers for the prosecution and from the lawyers for the defence. Then, the prosecution and defence witnesses gave evidence, and finally, the lawyers cross-examined the witnesses. After an adjournment, came the Second Hearing, the *actio secunda*—long concluding speeches from the lawyers of both sides, possibly followed by the introduction of further evidence. Finally, the verdict was given.

Unexpectedly, Cicero made only a very brief opening speech and immediately called his witnesses, presenting case after case of evidence against Verres. The trial lasted just nine days. Before the end of that time, Verres had fled from Rome.

In Verrem I was probably the speech Cicero prepared and delivered during the First Hearing. The First Hearing was never completed and the Second Hearing never took place. When Verres fled, the court passed sentence of exile and assessed damages against Verres.

In Verrem II was probably composed, perhaps as a rough draft, even before the trial began but Cicero never delivered it. After the trial, Cicero polished and published *In Verrem* II in the form of five speeches, each of which dealt with one specific type of charge against Verres. Although he never delivered these speeches, Cicero maintained the courtroom format, addressing the judges and defendant as if they were actually present.

The First Hearing Against Verres

THE SIGNIFICANCE OF THE CASE

inveteravit iam opinio perniciosa reipublicae nobisque periculosa—his iudiciis, quae nunc sunt, pecuniosum hominem, quamvis sit nocens, neminem posse damnari. nunc reus in iudicium adductus est C. Verres, homo vita atque factis omnium iam opinione 5
damnatus, pecuniae magnitudine sua spe absolutus. huic ego causae, iudices, cum summa voluntate et exspectatione populi Romani actor accessi, non ut augerem invidiam ordinis, sed ut infamiae communi succurrerem. adduxi enim hominem in quo recon- 10
ciliare existimationem iudiciorum amissam, redire in gratiam cum populo Romano, satis facere exteris nationibus possetis: depeculatorem aerarii, vexatorem Asiae, praedonem iuris urbani, labem atque perniciem provinciae Siciliae. de quo si vos severe ac religiose 15
iudicaveritis, auctoritas ea (quae in vobis remanere debet) haerebit.

   nunc autem homines in speculis sunt: observant quem ad modum sese unus quisque vestrum gerat in retinenda religione conservandisque legibus. hoc est 20
iudicium in quo vos de reo, populus Romanus de vobis iudicabit.

   CICERO, *IN VERREM* I.1.1-3; 16.46,47

The Significance of the Case

More than the judgement of one man is at stake in this case, Cicero claims. The court's credibility is at risk.

---

inveterasco, ascere, avi become established
opinio, onis, f a belief
perniciosus, a, um harmful
iudicium, i, n court, legal investigation
pecuniosus, a, um wealthy, rich
quamvis although
nocens, entis guilty
damno, are sentence, convict, condemn
C. = Gaius
reus, i, m defendant
6 *absolutus, a, um* set free, acquitted
causa, ae, f case
iudices judges, gentlemen of the jury
voluntas, atis, f goodwill, approval
exspectatio, onis, f interest
actor, oris, m prosecutor
accedo, ere, cessi come, appear
augeo, ere increase
invidia, ae, f unpopularity
ordo, ordinis, m rank; senatorial body
infamia, ae, f disgrace, dishonour
communis, e shared, general
10 *succurro, ere + dat.* assist in allaying
adduco, ere, duxi bring to justice, bring to trial
reconcilio, are restore
existimatio, onis, f good name, reputation
amitto, ere, misi, missus lose

gratia, ae, f favour
satis facio, facere give satisfaction, satisfy
exterus, a, um foreign
depeculator, oris, m robber, embezzler
aerarium, i, n public treasury
vexator, oris, m harasser
praedo, onis, m robber, plunderer
ius urbanum, iuris urbani, n city praetorship, city judicial system
labes, is, f disgrace, stain, blemish
pernicies, ei, f destruction, ruin
15 *religiose* conscientiously, scrupulously
iudico, are, avi + de + abl. pass judgement on
auctoritas, tatis, f authority, support
remaneo, ere stay, remain
haereo, ere stay, linger
specula, ae, f watchtower
homines in speculis sunt (i.e., the eyes of the world are on us)
observo, are observe, watch
quem ad modum how
unus quisque vestrum each one of you
se gerere conduct oneself
20 *retineo, ere* keep, maintain
religio, onis, f scrupulousness
conservo, are keep, observe
lex, legis, f law

The Charges Against Verres

Siciliam iste per triennium ita vexavit ac perdidit ut ea restitui in antiquum statum nullo modo possit. hoc praetore Siculi neque suas leges neque nostra senatus-consulta neque communia iura tenuerunt; tantum quisque habet in Sicilia quantum hominis avarissimi et libidinosissimi aut imprudentiam subterfugit aut satietati superfuit.

nulla res per triennium nisi ad nutum istius iudicata est; nulla res tam patria atque avita fuit quae non ab eo, imperio istius, abiudicaretur; innumerabiles pecuniae ex aratorum bonis novo nefarioque instituto coactae; socii fidelissimi in hostium numero existimati; cives Romani servilem in modum cruciati et necati; homines nocentissimi propter pecunias iudicio liberati, honestissimi atque integerrimi, absentes rei facti, indicta causa, damnati et eiecti; portus munitissimi, maximae tutissimaeque urbes, piratis praedonibusque patefactae; nautae militesque Siculorum, socii nostri atque amici, fame necati; classes optimae atque opportunissimae cum magna ignominia populi Romani amissae et perditae.

idem iste praetor monumenta antiquissima spoliavit nudavitque omnia. in stupris vero et flagitiis nefarias eius libidines commemorare pudore deterreor.

CICERO, *IN VERREM* I.4.12; 5.13-15

The Charges Against Verres

iste that fellow, the defendant: commonly used with derogatory intent
per triennium: Verres went to Sicily in 73 B.C. as propraetor or governor for one year. However, his term extended to three years because the revolt led by Spartacus made it impossible for Verres' successor to replace him.
vexo, are, avi devastate
perdo, ere, didi destroy
restituo, ere restore
status, us, m condition
praetor, oris, m praetor, governor
Siculus, i, m a Sicilian
senatus-consultum, i, n decree of the senate
ius, iuris, n legal rights
tantus...quantus as much...as
6 *libidinosus, a, um* licentious, wanton
imprudentia, ae, f attention, notice
subterfugo, ere, fugi escape
satietas, tatis, f sated appetite
supersum, esse, fui + dat. survive, am left
nutus, us, m nod, assent, compliance
res, rei, f: first used for case, lawsuit; in the next sentence, used for property
patrius, a, um father's
avitus, a, um grandfather's, ancestral
ab eo from him (i.e., from its proper owner)
10 *imperium, i, n* authority, rule
abiudico, are take away (by legal decision)
arator, oris, m landholder
bona, orum, n. pl. goods, possessions
nefarius, a, um wicked

institutum, i, n ordinance, decree: passed arbitrarily by a praetor (governor)
coactae = *coactae sunt*
cogo, ere, coegi, coactus force, extort
socius, i, m ally
in hostium numero existimati (sunt) were regarded as enemies
servilem in modum like slaves
crucio, are, avi, atus torture
neco, are, avi, atus kill
nocens, entis guilty
propter + acc. because of
15 *integer, gra, grum* honourable
absentes rei facti (sunt) were brought to trial in their absence
indictus, a, um untried, unheard
eicio, ere, eieci, eiectus banish
munitus, a, um fortified
praedo, onis, m robber
patefacio, ere, feci, factus throw open
fame necatus starved to death
classis, is, f fleet
opportunus, a, um valuable
20 *ignominia, ae, f* disgrace
spolio, are, avi rob, deprive
nudo, are, avi strip, lay bare
stuprum, i, n disgrace (esp., adultery)
vero indeed, in fact, truly
flagitium, i, n shameful crime
nefarius, a, um abominable
libido, inis, f wanton desire
commemoro, are repeat, relate
pudor, oris, m decency, sense of shame
deterreo, ere discourage, deter

The Second Hearing Against Verres

THE LOOTING OF ART TREASURES

venio nunc ad istius, quem ad modum ipse appellat, studium, ut amici eius, morbum et insaniam, ut Siculi, latrocinium. ego quo nomine appellem nescio. rem vobis proponam, vos eam suo, non nominis, pondere penditote. genus ipsum prius cognoscite, iudices; deinde fortasse non magno opere quaeretis quo id nomine appellandum putetis.

  nego in Sicilia tota, tam locupleti, tam vetere provincia, tot oppidis, tot familiis copiosis, ullum argenteum vas, ullum Corinthium aut Deliacum fuisse, ullam gemmam aut margaritam, quicquam ex auro aut ebore factum, signum ullum aeneum, marmoreum, eburneum, nego ullam picturam neque in tabula neque in textili, quin conquisierit, inspexerit, quod placitum sit abstulerit.

  magnum videor dicere. attendite etiam quem ad modum dicam. cum dico nihil istum eius modi rerum in tota provincia reliquisse, Latine me scitote, non accusatorie loqui. etiam planius: nihil in aedibus cuiusquam, ne in hospitis quidem, nihil in locis communibus, ne in fanis quidem, nihil apud Siculum, nihil apud civem Romanum, denique nihil istum, quod ad oculos animumque acciderit, neque privati neque publici neque profani neque sacri tota in Sicilia reliquisse.

        CICERO, *IN VERREM* II.iv.1.1-2

The Second Hearing Against Verres

The following selections are taken from the fourth in a series of five speeches Cicero prepared for the *actio secunda*. Each speech deals with a specific charge against Verres. This fourth speech presents evidence of Verres' looting of the art treasures of Sicily.

The Looting of Art Treasures

Because it is part of a larger speech, the fourth speech does not open with a formal exordium or introduction. Instead, Cicero moves quickly from the crimes listed in the third speech to those of the fourth.

---

iste that fellow, the defendant: commonly used with derogatory intent
quem ad modum as
appello, are name, call
studium, i, n favourite pursuit
ut as
morbus, i, m sickness, disease
Siculus, i, m a Sicilian
latrocinium, i, n highway robbery
nescio, ire do not know
propono, ere relate, set before
pondus, eris, n weight, value
5 *penditote = pendite*
pendo, ere weigh, judge
genus ipsum = genus ipsum criminis
genus, eris, n kind, sort, type
cognosco, ere learn
iudices judges, gentlemen of the jury
non magno opere quaeretis you will be at no great loss to know
appellandum = appellandum esse
puto, are think, consider
nego, are do not know
locuples, etis rich
vetus, eris old, venerable: Sicily was Rome's first province
oppidis, familiis: abl.
oppidum, i, n town
familiae, arum, f households, estates
copiosus, a, um rich
10 *argenteus, a, um* silver, of silver
vas, vasis, n vessel, dish, vase

Corinthium, Deliacum: Corinth and Delos (a small Greek island) were both famous for their bronze vessels
gemma, ae, f gem, engraved stone
margarita, ae, f pearl
quicquam = quidquam anything
aurum, i, n gold
ebur, oris, n ivory
signum, i, n statue
aeneus, a, um of bronze, bronze
marmoreus, a, um of marble, marble
eburneus, a, um of ivory, ivory
tabula, ae, f painting
textile, is, n tapestry, cloth
quin that...not
conquiro, ere, quisii hunt down
14 *quod placitum sit:* if he liked it
aufero, ferre, abstuli steal, take away
magnum dicere to exaggerate
attendo, ere attend to, listen, note
Latine me loqui scitote know I am speaking in plain Latin (i.e., speak the literal truth)
accusatorie as the prosecutor
planius = planius loquar
aedes, is, f. sing. temple; *f. pl.* house
20 *ne...quidem* not even
hospes, itis, m host
in locis communibus in public places
fanum, i, n temple, shrine
istum: subject of *reliquisse*
animus, i, m heart, attention
profanus, a, um secular

The Case of Heius' Chapel Ornaments

C. Heius est Mamertinus. huius domus est optima Messanae, notissima quidem certe, et nostris hominibus apertissima maximeque hospitalis. ea domus ante istius adventum ornata sic fuit ut urbi quoque esset ornamento. 5
  erat apud Heium sacrarium a maioribus traditum perantiquum, in quo signa pulcherrima quattuor summo artificio, summa nobilitate. unum Cupidinis marmoreum Praxiteli—nimirum didici etiam, dum in istum inquiro, artificum nomina. ex altera parte 10 Hercules egregie factus ex aere. is dicebatur esse Myronis, ut opinor. item ante hos deos erant arulae, quae cuivis religionem sacrarii significare possent. erant aenea duo praeterea signa, non maxima, verum eximia venustate, virginali habitu atque vestitu, quae manibus 15 sublatis sacra quaedam more Atheniensium virginum reposita in capitibus sustinebant. Canephoroe ipsae vocabantur; sed earum artificem—quem? quemnam? recte admones, Polyclitum esse dicebant. Messanam ut quisque nostrum venerat, haec visere solebat. om- 20 nibus haec ad visendum patebant cotidie; domus erat non domino magis ornamento quam civitati.

                    (continued on page 28)

The Case of Heius' Chapel Ornaments

Heius' private chapel with its art treasures was one of the tourist spots of Messana, Sicily—until Verres saw it!

C. = *Gaius*
Mamertinus citizen of Messana, a city in northeast Sicily
apertus, a, um open
adventus, us, m arrival
6 *sacrarium, i, n* shrine, chapel
maiores, um, m. pl. ancestors
perantiquus, a, um ancient
signum, i, n statue
artificium, i, n craftsmanship, skill
nobilitas, tatis, f artistic merit
marmoreus, a, um of marble, marble
Praxiteli by Praxiteles, a famous sculptor in Athens in the fourth century B.C. His statues were much admired and many Roman copies of his work still survive, including a Cupid (Vatican Museum).
nimirum of course
disco, ere, didici learn
dum...inquiro while I was investigating: referring to Cicero's tour of Sicily collecting evidence before the trial
10 *artificum nomina* the names of the artists: Romans were not supposed to admit to any expert knowledge of art and artists
ex altera parte opposite to it
egregie excellently, superbly
aes, aeris, n bronze
Myronis by Myron, a bronze sculptor of fifth-century Athens. One of his most famous is the *Discobolus* — the Discus Thrower.

ut opinor: again, rather than seem knowledgeable about art, Cicero pretends to express some doubt as to the identity of the artist
item also
arula, ae, f little altar
cuivis: dat. sg. of *quivis* to anyone
religio, ionis, f sanctity
aeneus, a, um of bronze, bronze
praeterea moreover
eximius, a, um special, remarkable
15 *venustas, tatis, f* charm, beauty
virginalis, e of a maiden
habitus, us, m appearance
vestitus, us, m dress, clothing
manibus sublatis with uplifted hands
sacra, n. pl. sacred objects
mos, moris, m fashion, custom
caput, itis, n head
Canephoroe: a Greek word "basket-carriers"
quem? quemnam? who was he? whom did they say he was? Another example of Cicero feigning ignorance or forgetfulness about artistic knowledge
recte admones you remind me well: Cicero suggests that his court secretary supplies him with the necessary information
Polyclitus: a famous sculptor and architect from Argos, in southern Greece, of the middle of the fifth century B.C.
20 *ut* whenever
viso, ere visit, go to see
pateo, ere lie open

haec omnia quae dixi signa, iudices, ab Heio e sacrario Verres abstulit; nullum, inquam, horum reliquit neque aliud ullum praeter unum pervetus ligneum, Bonam Fortunam, ut opinor; eam iste habere domi suae noluit.

pro deum hominumque fidem, quid hoc est? quae haec causa est? quae ista impudentia? quae dico signa, antequam abs te sublata sunt, Messanam cum imperio nemo venit quin viserit. tot praetores, tot consules in Sicilia cum in pace tum etiam in bello fuerunt, tot homines cuiusque modi—non loquor de integris, innocentibus, religiosis—tot cupidi, tot improbi, tot audaces, quorum nemo sibi tam vehemens, tam potens, tam nobilis visus est qui ex illo sacrario quicquam poscere aut tollere aut attingere auderet. Verres quod ubique erit pulcherrimum auferet? nihil habere cuiquam praeterea licebit? tot domus locupletissimas istius domus una capiet? idcirco nemo superiorum attigit, ut hic tolleret?

sed quid ego tam vehementer invehor? verbo uno repellar. "emi," inquit. di immortales! praeclaram defensionem! mercatorem in provinciam cum imperio ac securibus misimus, omnia qui signa, tabulas pictas, omne argentum, aurum, ebur, gemmas coemeret, nihil cuiquam relinqueret!

CICERO, *IN VERREM* II.iv.2.3-8

25 *praeter* + *acc.* except
pervetus, eris very old
ligneum (signum) wooden statue: the earliest Greek statues were made of wood
pro + *acc. of exclamation* by the..., in the name of...
deum = *deorum*
causa, ae, f case
impudentia, ae, f shamelessness
30 *cum imperio nemo* no governor: *imperium* was the military authority granted the governor by the state
quin who ... not
praetores, consules a propraetor governed a province at peace; a pro-consul governed one that needed the presence of many troops
cum...tum not only...but also
quisque, quaeque, quidque each
integer, gra, grum honest, sincere
religiosus, a, um conscientious
cupidus, a, um greedy
improbus, a, um immoral
35 *sibi...visus est* saw himself, thought himself

vehemens, entis determined, strong
potens, entis powerful
quicquam = *quidquam* anything
posco, ere demand
attingo, ere touch, lay hands on
qui...auderet: rel. cl. of characteristic as to dare
audeo, ere dare
quod = *id quod*
ubique everywhere
aufero, ferre steal, carry off
cuiquam praeterea to anyone but him
locuples, pletis rich, wealthy
domus: first used in acc. pl., then in nom. sg.
40 *idcirco* on that account, for that reason
superiorum of his predecessors
invehor, i attack
repello, ere drive back, drive away
praeclarus, a, um outstanding, excellent
45 *securis, is, f* axe; supreme power: the highest Roman officials had *secures* or *fasces* (bundle of rods) as insignia of high rank
coemo, ere buy up

The Peroration

nunc te, Iuppiter Optime Maxime, cuiusque sanctissimum et pulcherrimum simulacrum Syracusis sustulit; teque, Minerva, quam item expilavit, cum Syracusis omnia praeter tectum et parietes abstulit; teque, Hercules; ceteros item deos deasque omnes imploro et obtestor, quorum templis et religionibus iste nefario quodam furore et audacia instinctus bellum sacrilegum semper impiumque habuit:

  ut, si in hoc reo atque in hac causa omnia mea consilia ad salutem sociorum, dignitatem rei publicae, fidem meum spectaverunt, atque si eius omnia sunt inaudita et singularia facinora sceleris, audaciae, perfidiae, libidinis, avaritiae, crudelitatis, exitus dignus vita atque factis vestro iudicio consequatur, utique res publica meaque fides una hac accusatione mea contenta sit, mihique posthac bonos potius defendere liceat quam improbos accusare necesse sit.

CICERO, *IN VERREM* II.v.72.184, 186, 188-189

The Peroration

From presenting evidence of Verres' looting of the art treasures of Sicily, Cicero moves on to the fifth and final section of his second speech. Since it is the last section of the *actio secunda*, Cicero ends with a formal summing up, *peroratio*.

Syracusae, arum, f. pl. Syracuse, a chief city of Sicily which was plundered by Verres
expilo, are, avi rob, plunder
praeter + acc. except
tectum, i, n roof
paries, ietis, m wall
5 *ceteros item deos...:* this concludes Cicero's long catalogue (here omitted) in which he invokes many deities whose worship Verres defiled; each name would remind the judges of a case already cited as evidence against Verres
imploro, are call upon with tears, beseech, implore
obtestor, ari call as witnesses
religio, onis, f worship
nefarius, a, um abominable, impious
furor, oris, m madness
instinctus, a, um incited, impelled
bellum habuit + gen. wage war against
reus, i, m defendant, accused
consilium, i, n deliberation
10 *salus, utis, f* welfare, interests
socius, i, m ally
dignitas, tatis, f honour
res publica, rei publicae, f state

fides, fidei, f honesty, honour
specto, are, avi look to
inauditus, a, um unheard of, unusual
singularius, a, um extraordinary
facinus, oris, n crime, villainy
scelus, eris, n wickedness
perfidia, ae, f treachery
libido, inis, f lust
ut...exitus...consequatur: indirect command introduced by "*imploro et obtestor*" (line 6) that destruction may follow
exitus, us, m an end, destruction
dignus, a, um + abl. as befits
vestro iudicio as a result of your verdict
consequor, i follow
utique and that
15 *una hac accusatione mea* with this one prosecution by me: Cicero preferred to be a defence lawyer; earlier in the case he had mentioned that only his friendship with many Sicilians and the enormity of Verres' crimes persuaded him to act as a prosecutor
posthac after this
boni, orum, m. pl. good men
potius...quam rather ... than
improbi, orum, m. pl. evil men

THE PRACTICAL VIEW

The Conscientious Governor

Initial Questions

The Need for Provincial Reform
1. What are the details of the emperor's advice concerning Pliny's administrative problem?
2. What aspect of Pliny's mission to Bithynia does Trajan emphasize here? What does this emphasis reveal about Trajan? about Pliny?

An Aqueduct in Nicomedia
1. Many of Pliny's letters reveal his tireless efforts to improve the amenities of life in the province. Yet these same letters expose the deficiencies of previous administrations. What do you see as the reasons for the problems that confront Pliny in Nicomedia?
2. Why do you think Pliny does not abandon the entire project?
3. How does Pliny try to influence Trajan into accepting his plan to proceed?
4. What problem does Trajan think is greater than that of providing an adequate water supply?
5. Where does Trajan express his impatience with Pliny for failing to attack that problem?

A Sewer for Amastris
1. Find all the words that indicate that Pliny, a former member of the Tiber River Commission, is scandalized by the situation in Amastris.
2. What do you think Trajan's answer will be? Why? Now read Trajan's letter. To what extent were you able to anticipate Trajan's grasp of the issues?

A Theatre and Gymnasium for Nicaea
1. List all the indications that suggest that Nicaea has suffered from either administrative inefficiency or dishonesty.
2. What three solutions to the problem of the gymnasium does Pliny consider? Which would you pursue and why?
3. What reason does Trajan give for not providing Pliny with an answer to his building problems? What reason does he give for not sending an engineer?

Party Favours
1. What two dangers does Pliny fear will result from the practice of holding large celebratory parties?
2. To what extent would Trajan's answer help Pliny?
3. What aspect of Pliny's mission to Bithynia does Trajan emphasize here?

The Disreputable Governor

Initial Questions

Significance of the Case
1. What view of the Senate's judicial fairness has become generally accepted at Rome? Why does Cicero feel that the Senate now has a chance to redeem its reputation?
2. Why, according to Cicero in this part of his speech, did he accept the case?
3. Find two rhetorical devices Cicero uses to persuade the judges. Analyze each carefully in its context and indicate how and why it would be effective. To what extent would each be effective in a courtroom today?

The Charges Against Verres
1. What do you think is the worst charge against Verres? Why? Which does Cicero seem to feel is the worst? Can you suggest why Cicero feels that way?
2. What rhetorical devices does Cicero use in this selection to make his indignation plain?

The Looting of Art Treasures
1. What different words do different people use to describe Verres' interest in acquiring art treasures? Why do you think Cicero records these different views?
2. What is the rhetorical effect of the long sentence that makes up paragraph two of this selection?

The Case of Heius' Chapel Ornaments
1. Why do you think Cicero describes the ornaments and names the artists or craftsmen?
2. What, in Cicero's opinion, makes this theft especially blameworthy?
3. Explain how Cicero uses sarcasm or irony as weapons in his attack on Verres.

Peroration
1. Is Cicero's appeal in his conclusion mainly logical or mainly emotional, or is it both?
2. Consider to what extent this passage is effective as a conclusion to the court case against Verres.

Discussion Questions

1. Reread Pliny's advice to Maximus on Maximus becoming a governor (page 4). Compare Pliny's advice with his own deliberations and motives as revealed in his correspondence with Trajan. To what extent do you think Pliny practises what he preaches?
2. With regard to provincial policy, many Romans viewed themselves as protectors and benefactors. What material benefits of Romanization do the Pliny-Trajan letters reveal? What administrative benefits? What severe limitations of the system?
3. What indications do Pliny's letters give that he is writing to a superior? What indications are there that Trajan views Pliny as more than simply a civil servant?
4. Pliny was in Bithynia for just under two years. During this time, he asked the emperor's advice in some forty letters. Pliny has been criticized for his frequently

unnecessary desire for consultation. Re-examine the pairs of letters in this section and determine to what extent you feel Pliny was justified in seeking advice in each case.
5. Find a modern example of a civil servant's report to his/her superior. How does it compare with Pliny's reports? What do the differences tell you about differences in administrative styles and organizations?
6. Fully discuss the picture of Verres as governor that emerges from the selections you have read. Can you suggest a modern counterpart to Verres?
7. Compare and contrast ancient and modern methods of exposing corruption in government and public life.
8. Discuss fully the persuasive techniques that Cicero uses. Find a transcript of a famous modern trial. Compare the prosecutor's style of presenting the case with that of Cicero.

Further Reading

Trajan tells Pliny why he has been sent to Bithynia: (a) to make clear that the welfare of the province is a concern of the emperor and his chosen representative, and (b) to scrutinize the accounts: Pliny, *Epistulae* X.18.

Trajan refuses Pliny's request to establish a fire-fighting brigade on the grounds that Bithynia has a history of such organizations becoming a focal point for political disorder: Pliny, *Epistulae* X.34.

Pliny writes to Trajan suggesting that Byzantium could save money by writing a letter of allegiance to the emperor rather than by sending an embassy every year to Rome at great public expense. Trajan dryly agrees that the use of the imperial mail not only would adequately fulfil Byzantium's duty to him, but also would be much more economical: Pliny, *Epistulae* X.43, 44.

Trajan, in replying to a problem involving the emperor's statue and dishonest building contractors, reminds Pliny that he refuses to terrorize people into revering him, no matter what precedents previous emperors had established: Pliny, *Epistulae* X.82.

Pliny writes to Trajan requesting advice on how to deal with the Christians. Trajan's counsel includes a caveat against using anonymously given names as legal evidence: Pliny, *Epistulae* X.96, 97.

In his story of Nero and Agrippina, Tacitus describes an emperor's notorious murder of his mother: Tacitus, *Annals* XIV.3, 5, 8.

Cicero presents further evidence against Verres: The Case of Pamphilus' Cups: *In Verrem* II.iv.14. 32; The Case of the Temple of Hercules: *In Verrem* II.iv.43. 94-96; The Looting of Syracuse: *In Verrem* II.iv.52-67.

Cicero, *pater patriae*, saves the state from ruin at the hands of Catiline who attempted to overthrow the government: Sallust, *Catiline* 46.

Sallust describes a debate in the Senate over the type of punishment to be given the captured Catilinarian conspirators: Sallust, *Catiline* 50-53.

Cicero demands the death penalty for the Catilinarian prisoners who had conspired to overthrow the state: Cicero, *In Catilinam* IV.11, 12, 18-19.

THE PATRIOTIC VIEW

Statue of a Roman patrician holding busts of his ancestors. One of the old Roman virtues was respect for one's ancestors who had made Rome great. (Rome, Capitoline Museum)

In Praise of Roman Rule

"terram vestram ceterorumque Gallorum ingressi sunt duces imperatoresque Romani nulla cupidine, sed maioribus vestris invocantibus, quos discordiae usque ad exitium fatigabant, et acciti auxilio Germani sociis pariter atque hostibus servitutem imposuerant. nec ideo Rhenum insedimus ut Italiam tueremur, sed ne quis alius Ariovistus regno Galliarum potiretur. eadem semper causa Germanis transcendendi in Gallias, libido atque avaritia et mutandae sedis amor, ut relictis paludibus et solitudinibus suis fecundissimum hoc solum vosque ipsos possiderent.

regna bellaque per Gallias semper fuere donec in nostrum ius concederetis. nos, quamquam totiens lacessiti, iure victoriae id solum vobis addidimus, quo pacem tueremur. nam neque quies gentium sine armis neque arma sine stipendiis neque stipendia sine tributis haberi queunt; cetera in communi sita sunt. ipsi plerumque legionibus nostris praesidetis, ipsi has aliasque provincias regitis; nihil separatum clausumve.

(continued on page 38)

In Praise of Roman Rule

Taking advantage of the confusion with the death of the Emperor Vitellius and refusing to acknowledge Vespasian as the new Emperor, some of the tribes in Gaul rebelled, assisted by some of the Roman legions stationed in that province (A.D. 69-70). In this passage from Tacitus, Petilius Cerialis, a Roman general, has just entered the now subdued colony of the Treviri on the borders of Germany. He addresses the first and sixteenth Roman legions who, confronted with the results of their treachery, are stricken with shame. In this selection, Cerialis reminds his listeners of the advantages of having the Romans in Gaul.

---

cupido, inis, f greed, desire for power
maiores, um, m. pl. ancestors
invoco, are call for help
usque ad exitium to death, to point of collapse
fatigo, are exhaust, weary
accio, ire, ivi, itus summon, call on
socius, i, m ally
5 *pariter atque* as well as, equally
hostis, is, m enemy
impono, ere, posui impose
ideo therefore
Rhenus, i, m the Rhine
insido, ere, sedi occupy
tueor, tueri guard, protect
Ariovistus: a German king whose occupation of Gallic territory on the border between Gaul and Germany led to Julius Caesar's first campaign in Gaul, 58 B.C.
potior, iri + abl. get possession of
causa transcendendi reason for crossing
libido, inis, f lust, passion
avaritia, ae, f greed
mutandae sedis amor a yearning to change homes

10 *palus, udis, f* swamp, bog
solitudo, inis, f desert
fecundus, a, um rich
solum, i, n soil, ground
regnum, i, n kingdom
bellum, i, n war
fuere = fuerunt
donec until
ius, iuris, n law, order
concedo, ere submit, yield
totiens frequently, so often
lacesso, ere, ivi, itus irritate, exasperate
quo pacem tueremur the cost of our preserving the peace
15 *gens, tis, f* tribe
stipendium, i, n military service
tributum, i, n tribute, tax
queo, quire + inf. be able
sino, ere, sivi, situs permit, leave
plerumque generally, often
praesideo, ere + dat. preside over, manage, direct
rego, ere rule
separatus, a, um separate, apart
clausus, a, um excluded, blocked off
-ve or

37

et laudatorum principum usus ex aequo quamvis procul agentibus: saevi proximis ingruunt. quo modo sterilitatem aut nimios imbris et cetera naturae mala, ita luxum vel avaritiam dominantium tolerate. vitia erunt, donec homines, sed neque haec continua et meliorum interventu pensantur.

pulsis—quod di prohibeant—Romanis, quid aliud quam bella omnium inter se gentium existent? octingentorum annorum fortuna disciplinaque compages haec coaluit, quae convelli sine exitio convellentium non potest.

proinde pacem et urbem, quam victi victoresque eodem iure obtinemus, amate colite; moneant vos utriusque fortunae documenta ne contumaciam cum pernicie quam obsequium cum securitate malitis."

TACITUS, *HISTORIES* IV.73-74

20 *laudo, are, avi, atus* praise
princeps, cipis, m emperor
usus (habetis) + *gen.* you enjoy the advantages of
ex aequo equally
quamvis procul agentibus although you live far away (from Rome)
saevi = principes saevi
proximus, a, um living nearby
ingruo, ere + *dat.* fall on, attack
quo modo...ita as...so
sterilitas, tatis, f barrenness
nimius, a, um too much
imber, bris, m rain
malum, i, n evil
luxus, us, m excess
vel or
vitium, i, n imperfection, fault
donec as long as, while
continuus, a, um perpetual
melior, melius better
interventus, us, m intervention
25 *penso, are* counterbalance, compensate

pulsis Romanis: abl. abs. with conditional value if the Romans are driven back, defeated
prohibeo, ere prevent, forbid
existo, ere emerge, appear, exist
octingenti, ae, a eight hundred
compages, ei, f structure
coalesco, alescere, alui take root, grow together
convello, ere destroy
exitium, i, n destruction, ruin
31 *proinde* therefore
obtineo, ere possess
colo, ere cherish, love
moneo, ere warn
utriusque fortunae of good and bad fortune
documentum, i, n lesson, example
contumacia, ae, f obstinacy, defiance
pernicies, ei, f destruction, ruin
malo...quam... I prefer...to...
obsequium, i, n obedience, submission
securitas, tatis, f security

A Thanksgiving Ode

nunc est bibendum, nunc pede libero
pulsanda tellus, nunc Saliaribus
   ornare pulvinar deorum
      tempus erat dapibus, sodales.

antehac nefas depromere Caecubum   5
cellis avitis, dum Capitolio
   regina dementes ruinas
      funus et imperio parabat

contaminato cum grege turpium
morbo virorum, quidlibet impotens   10
   sperare fortunaque dulci
      ebria. sed minuit furorem

vix una sospes navis ab ignibus,
mentemque lymphatam Mareotico
   redegit in veros timores   15
      Caesar, ab Italia volantem

        (continued on page 42)

A Thanksgiving Ode

METRE: ALCAIC

Horace celebrates the suicide of Cleopatra in 30 B.C., a year after the battle in which Octavian (soon to become the Emperor Augustus) defeated the fleets of Cleopatra and Mark Antony. In Roman eyes, the war had not been a civil one. Octavian, champion of the West, had defeated Cleopatra, symbol of the barbarous East. Notice that Horace never mentions the Cleopatra-Antony liaison.

---

tellus, uris, f land, ground
Saliaribus...dapibus with sumptuous feasts: The Salii were priests whose banquets were known for their lavishness
pulvinar, aris, n couch of the gods, cushioned seat
pulvinar deorum: the thanksgiving banquet was served to the images of the gods placed on richly cushioned couches
tempus erat it is the time: the imperf. is used to indicate a fact already in existence
sodalis, is, m or f intimate friend, comrade
5 *nefas, n. indecl.* contrary to divine law, sin
depromo, ere to bring down: wine was stored in *amphorae* in the attics to mellow in the smoke rising from the hearth below
Caecubum Caecuban wine: Caecubum was an area in Latium, famous for its wine
cellis avitis from ancestral storerooms (i.e., the wine was put up by their ancestors)
Capitolio...et imperio for Rome and for the empire: the Capitoline Hill on which stood the Temple of Jupiter was a symbol for Rome
regina, ae, f queen: a word detested by the Romans

demens, entis insane, mad
funus, eris, n death
contaminatus, a, um polluted, defiled
grex, gregis, m flock, herd
turpis, e disgraceful, foul
10 *morbus, i, m* disease, immorality
quidlibet impotens sperare reckless enough to hope for anything (i.e., Cleopatra's ambition of marrying Antony and becoming ruler of Rome)
fortuna: abl.
minuo, ere, ui curtail, diminish
sospes, sospitis saved, unharmed
ab ignibus: in fact, Cleopatra's ships withdrew earlier in the battle and escaped to Alexandria; Antony's ships were burned except for his own which he had had equipped with sails
lymphatus, a, um raving, maddened
Mareotico with Egyptian wine: Mareota was a lake in Egypt
15 *redigo, ere, egi* redirect
Caesar: subject of *redegit* (i.e., Octavian)
volo, are fly, flee
volantem = *Cleopatram volantem*

remis adurgens, accipiter velut
molles columbas aut leporem citus
   venator in campis nivalis
      Haemoniae, daret ut catenis   20

fatale monstrum. quae generosius
perire quaerens nec muliebriter
   expavit ensem nec latentes
      classe cita reparavit oras;

ausa et iacentem visere regiam   25
vultu sereno, fortis et asperas
   tractare serpentes, ut atrum
      corpore combiberet venenum,

deliberata morte ferocior;
saevis Liburnis scilicet invidens   30
   privata deduci superbo
      non humilis mulier triumpho.

      HORACE, ODES I.37

remis adurgens pursuing in ships: in fact, Octavian didn't follow to Egypt until the next year
accipiter, tris, m falcon, hawk
velut just like
mollis, e soft, tender
lepus, oris, m hare
citus, a, um fast, swift
nivalis, e snowy: winter was the hunting season
20 *Haemonia, ae, f* Thessaly
daret ut = ut daret: purpose clause
catena, ae, f chain
fatalis, e deadly
quae she (i.e., Cleopatra)
generosius: comparative degree more nobly
muliebriter like a woman
expavesco, ere, pavi dread, fear
ensis, is, m sword, dagger: Cleopatra's first attempt at suicide was with a dagger
latentes...oras hidden shores: perhaps referring to a plan of escape via the Red Sea
classis, is, f fleet
reparo, are, avi seek, head for
25 *ausa = ausa est*

audeo, ere, ausus sum dare
et = etiam
iacens, entis ruined, lying in ruins
viso, ere gaze upon
regia, ae, f royal palace
vultus, us, m face, countenance
asper, era, erum poisonous, deadly
tracto, are handle
combibo, ere drink in, swallow
deliberata morte as she decided on death
30 *saevis Liburnis* by the savage Liburnians: perhaps referring to a captured Cleopatra's transfer to Rome by Liburnian ship; the Liburnians were famous for their small, fast ships which Octavian made use of in the Battle of Actium in which he defeated Antony and Cleopatra
scilicet no doubt, doubtlessly
invidens, entis scorning
privatus, a, um as a private citizen (i.e., deprived of her royal status)
deduci: present infinitive passive, direct object of invidens to be led (to Rome)
superbo triumpho: abl. of manner or dat. of interest

REGULUS: A MODEL ROMAN

caelo tonantem credidimus Iovem
regnare: praesens divus habebitur
   Augustus adiectis Britannis
      imperio gravibusque Persis.

milesne Crassi coniuge barbara   5
turpis maritus vixit et hostium —
   pro curia inversique mores! —
      consenuit socerorum in armis

sub rege Medo, Marsus et Apulus,
anciliorum et nominis et togae   10
   oblitus aeternaeque Vestae,
      incolumi Iove et urbe Roma?

hoc caverat mens provida Reguli
dissentientis condicionibus
   foedis et exemplo trahentis   15
      perniciem veniens in aevum,

      (continued on page 46)

Regulus: a Model Roman

METRE: ALCAIC

Regulus is held up as the ideal of the old Roman virtues: his moral strength and resolution as a captive of Carthage are contrasted with the disgraceful behaviour of the present-day Roman soldiers captured by the armies of Parthia, an ancient country located where Iran is today.

---

tonantem because he thunders
habebitur shall be held, shall be considered
divus, i, m a god
adiectis Britannis...gravibusque Persis: abl. abs.
adicio, ere, ieci, iectus add
imperium, i, n empire
gravis, e troublesome, dreaded
5 *Crassus*: the commander of the Roman army that was disastrously defeated in 53 B.C. by the Parthians
coniuge barbara with a foreign wife: many of the captured Roman soldiers later married Parthian wives and even fought in the Parthian army against the Romans
turpis, e disgraceful, shameful
hostium...socerorum of enemy fathers-in-law
pro: *interjection* by
curia, ae, f Senate house; symbol of Roman power
inversus, a, um overthrown, altered
mores, um, m. pl. character, ways
consenesco, ere, senui grow old: the disaster occurred in 53 B.C. and this ode was composed about 27 B.C.
rex, regis, m king: a word and concept hated by the Romans
Medus, a, um Median, of Media, of Persia, of Parthia
Marsus et Apulus: typify the best of Roman soldiers
10 *anciliorum, nominis, togae, Vestae*: gen. governed by *oblitus*
ancile, is, m or *ancilium, i, n* shield: Jupiter sent this shield from heaven in the reign of Numa, an early king of Rome; the prosperity of Rome was thought to depend on its preservation
oblitus, a, um + gen. forgetful of
Vesta, ae, f Vesta: goddess of the hearth; Vestal Virgins guarded the sacred fire in the temple of Vesta in the Roman Forum; the unquenched fire symbolized the permanence of Rome
incolumis, e intact, unharmed
Iove: Jupiter's temple was on the Capitoline
caveo, ere, cavi guard against
providus, a, um farseeing
Regulus Marcus Atilius Regulus was a Roman general who fought against Carthage in the First Punic War. He was captured by the Carthaginians and in 250 B.C. he was sent to Rome to arrange an exchange of prisoners. He urged the Roman Senate not to accept terms but to let the prisoners die in Carthage. He himself returned to Carthage to face torture and death for failing in his mission.
dissentientis + dat. *modifying Reguli* disagreeing with
condicio, onis, f conditions, terms
15 *foedus, a, um* shameful, disgraceful
exemplum, i, n precedent
traho, ere infer
pernicies, ei, f ruin, destruction
veniens in aevum for the coming era, for the age to come

si non periret immiserabilis
captiva pubes. "signa ego Punicis
   adfixa delubris et arma
      militibus sine caede" dixit   20

"derepta vidi; vidi ego civium
retorta tergo bracchia libero
   portasque non clausas et arva
      Marte coli populata nostro.

auro repensus scilicet acrior   25
miles redibit. flagitio additis
   damnum: neque amissos colores
      lana refert medicata fuco,

nec vera virtus, cum semel excidit,
curat reponi deterioribus.   30
   si pugnat extricata densis
      cerva plagis, erit ille fortis

qui perfidis se credidit hostibus,
et Marte Poenos proteret altero,
   qui lora restrictis lacertis   35
      sensit iners timuitque mortem.

hic, unde vitam sumeret inscius,
pacem duello miscuit. o pudor!
   o magna Karthago, probrosis
      altior Italiae ruinis!"   40

      (continued on page 48)

immiserabilis, e unpitied
pubes, is, f young men: a collective noun here referring to young soldiers
signa, orum, n. pl. the standards: referring to the legionary standards lost in the battle
Punicus, a, um Punic, Carthaginian
adfigo, ere, fixi, fixus fix to, fasten to: it was customary in ancient times to hang such trophies up as thank offerings to the gods
delubrum, i, n shrine, temple
arma, orum, n. pl. weapons, armour
caedes, is, f bloodshed
dereptus, a, um + dat. snatched from
civium = civium Romanorum the milites have lost the right to be called soldiers
retortus, a, um twisted back, twisted behind
bracchia: acc. pl. object of *vidi*
bracchium, i, n arms
libero: transferred epithet, an adjective that grammatically modifies one word (*tergo*), but in meaning relates to another (*civium*)
arvum, i, n ploughed land, field
Marte nostro by our warfare: Mars was the god of war
colo, ere cultivate
populor, ari, populatus ravage, lay waste
repensus, a, um ransomed, redeemed
scilicet doubtless: ironic tone
flagitium, i, n shame, disgrace

addo, ere add
damnum, i, n loss, waste (i.e., of the ransom money)
lana, ae, f wool
refero, ferre get back, regain
medicatus, a, um steeped, stained
fucus, i, m dye
excido, ere, cidi vanish
30 *deterioribus* to/on the weaklings, degenerates
si pugnat...cerva...erit ille fortis if a doe...puts ups a fight, then will that man be brave who...
extrico, are, avi, atus disentangle, set free
densus, a, um thickly meshed
cerva, ae, f doe, deer
plaga, ae, f hunting-net
perfidus, a, um treacherous, faithless
Marte altero in new wars, in some other war
protero, ere crush, trample
35 *lorum, i, n* thong
restringo, ere, strinxi, strictus bind back
lacertus, i, m arm
iners, ertis tamely, lifelessly, passively
sumo, ere take, assume
inscius, a, um unaware
duello: an archaism for *bello: bellum, i, n* war
misceo, ere, miscui mix, confuse
pudor, oris, m shame
probrosus, a, um shameful, disgraceful
40 *altior* made greater, elevated (by)
ruinis: abl. by the ruins

fertur pudicae coniugis osculum
parvosque natos ut capitis minor
   ab se removisse et virilem
      torvus humi posuisse vultum,

donec labantes consilio patres   45
firmaret auctor numquam alias dato,
   interque maerentes amicos
      egregius properaret exsul.

atque sciebat quae sibi barbarus
tortor pararet; non aliter tamen   50
   dimovit obstantes propinquos
      et populum reditus morantem

quam si clientum longa negotia
diiudicata lite relinqueret,
   tendens Venafranos in agros   55
      aut Lacedaemonium Tarentum.

        HORACE, *ODES* III.5

fertur he is said, people say that he
pudicus, a, um chaste
coniunx, iugis, m and f husband, wife
osculum, i, n kiss
ut capitis minor as one deprived of his civil rights: *caput* refers to a Roman's personal and political rights
virilis, e manly
torvus fiercely
humi on the ground
vultus, us, m face, countenance
5 *donec* until
labens, entis shaking, wavering
consilium, i, n advice
patres the senators
firmo, are strengthen
auctor by his influence
alias before or since
maerens, entis mourning, sorrowful
egregius, a, um glorious, outstanding, uncommon
propero, are hurry, hasten
exsul, sulis, m and f exile

50 *tortor, oris, m* torturer
non aliter tamen...negotia = *tamen dimovit...propinquos et populum...non aliter quam si, diiudicata lite, relinqueret negotia*
dimoveo, ere, movi move aside
obstans, antis blocking the way
propinquus, i, m relative, kinsman
reditus, us, m return
morans, antis delaying
non aliter quam si just as if, as calmly as if
clientum = *clientium*: gen. pl.: referring to Regulus' duty as patron to assist his clients in legal affairs
diiudico, are, avi, atus decide, settle
lis, litis, f lawsuit, case in court
55 *tendo, ere* head for, stretch out
Venafranus, a, um of Venafrum, a town southeast of Rome, which was a popular holiday resort
Lacedaemonium Tarentum: Tarentum, a Spartan colony in south Italy, was another popular resort in Horace's time

THE PATRIOTIC VIEW

Initial Questions

In Praise of Roman Rule
1. What timeless arguments for foreign intervention does Cerialis here use to justify the Roman presence in Gaul? What, in return, has Rome gained?
2. Tacitus was trained as an orator. Consider the extent to which he has Cerialis use rhetorical techniques to persuade his audience to his point of view.

A Thanksgiving Ode
1. The Romans saw Cleopatra as a symbol of the soft, luxurious East. Study the contexts where Horace encourages this popular imperial propaganda. Examine in particular specific words with hidden or double connotations. Notice the juxtaposition with symbols sacred to Rome.
2. Examine the thought-sequence in the poem. Where does the shift in Horace's attitude to Cleopatra begin? Consider why Horace not only makes this change, but even makes it the climax of his ode.

Regulus, a Model Roman
1. Carefully study the thought-sequence in this poem. Consider the contrast between Regulus and those Horace considers unworthy of the name Roman. How does Horace maintain unity in such a lengthy poem?
2. The Regulus story, along with several other models of Roman patriotism, was a set-piece for orators by Horace's day. How does Horace rescue the story from being trite and hackneyed?

Discussion Questions

1. In the poems in this section, Horace's voice is that of a national poet of Rome. Discuss the extent to which these poems set forth the political, religious, and moral issues of the day.
2. Cerialis and Regulus each gives us patriotic views of Roman rule. What qualities does each value as justifying the destiny of Rome and its citizens to rule? What negative qualities does each either admit or warn against?

Further Reading

Livy relates the story of Coriolanus to illustrate the great old Roman virtue of *pietas*—loyalty, faithfulness, and duty to the gods, the family, and the state: Livy, *Ab Urbe Condita* II.40.

Vergil extols the virtues of Italy—its land, its produce, its cities, and its great leaders, greatest of which is Augustus Caesar: Vergil, *Georgics* II.136-176.

Sallust recalls the strengths of the old Roman character that made Rome great: Sallust, *Catiline* 7-9.

Horace extols Roman *virtus: dulce et decorum est pro patria mori*. Young Roman men should learn courage from the dangers and hardships of war: Horace, *Odes* III.2.

Horace depicts the state as a ship, the civil wars as a storm at sea, and the hope of a new regime of peace as the safe harbour: Horace, *Odes* I.14.

THE CRITICAL VIEW

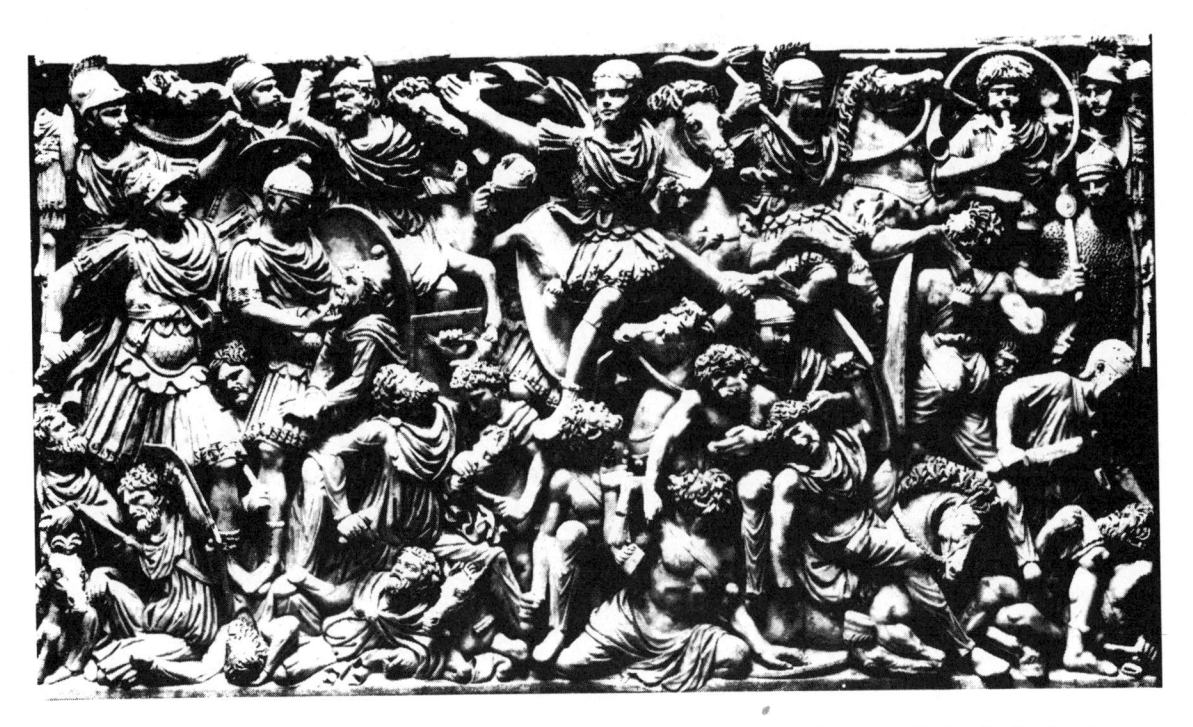

Part of a marble sarcophagus depicting the Romans fighting the barbarians. Only the barbarians are represented as dying. (Rome, Museo Nazionale Romano)

The Disastrous Years

opus adgredior opimum casibus, atrox proeliis, discors seditionibus, ipsa etiam pace saevum. quattuor principes ferro interempti; trina bella civilia, plura externa ac plerumque permixta; prosperae in Oriente, adversae in Occidente res; turbatum Illyricum, Galliae 5 nutantes, perdomita Britannia et statim omissa.

   iam vero Italia novis cladibus vel post longam saeculorum seriem repetitis adflicta. haustae aut obrutae urbes, fecundissima Campaniae ora; et urbs incendiis vastata, consumptis antiquissimis delubris, 10 ipso Capitolio civium manibus incenso.

                        (continued on page 54)

The Disastrous Years

This passage comes from Tacitus' introduction to his *Histories* which cover the years A.D. 69-96. Writing in a rare age of liberty, he can, he says, write the truth of the past years of chaos and terror.

---

opus adgredior I come to a time in history
opimus, a, um rich
casus, us, m disaster
atrox, atrocis terrible, cruel
proelium, i, n battle
discors, cordis discordant
seditio, onis, f civil insurrection, civil strife
quattuor principes the four emperors: Galba was murdered during Otho's coup; Otho committed suicide during Vitellius' coup; Vitellius was killed when Vespasian took Rome (all in A.D. 69). Domitian (A.D. 81-96), who at first continued the fair rule of Vespasian and Titus, became a cruel tyrant in later years and was murdered.
interempti = *interempti sunt*
interimo, imere, emi, emptus destroy, kill
trini, ae, a three
trina bella civilia: Otho against Vitellius, Vitellius against Vespasian, and perhaps Domitian in the German revolt or Galba against Otho
externus, a, um foreign
plerumque often, generally
permixtus, a, um at the same time
prosperae in Oriente...res good fortune in the East: the Romans were successful against the Jews
5 *adversae res* misfortune
Occidens, entis, m the West
turbatus, a, um disturbed
Illyricum, i, n Illyria, a Roman province on the Adriatic

Galliae, f. pl. the Roman provinces of Gaul
nuto, are waver
perdomo, are, ui, itus tame, subdue
omitto, ere, misi, missus neglect
perdomita...omissa: Britain was conquered by the Roman armies led by Agricola (A.D. 77-84); the Romans withdrew from parts of Britain later in Domitian's reign
iam vero indeed, finally
novus, a, um unknown before
clades, is, f disaster
saeculum, i, n age, generation
series, ei, f series, succession
repeto, ere, ivi, itus repeat
adflictus, a, um shattered, damaged
haustae...ora: referring to the volcanic activity of Vesuvius
haurio, ire, hausi, haustus swallow up, destroy
obruo, ere, rui, rutus overturn, bury
fecundus, a, um rich, fertile
ora, ae, f shore
urbs...incenso: referring to the great fire in Rome in A.D. 69 which started during the war between the supporters of Vitellius and those of Vespasian
10 *vasto, are, avi, atus* devastate
consumptis...delubris, capitolio...incenso: abl. absolutes
delubrum, i, n shrine, temple
Capitolium, i, n the Capitoline Hill, symbol of Rome

pollutae caerimoniae, magna adulteria. plenum exiliis mare, infecti caedibus scopuli. atrocius in urbe saevitum; nobilitas, opes, omissi gestique honores pro crimine et ob virtutes certissimum exitium. nec minus praemia delatorum invisa quam scelera, cum alii sacerdotia et consulatus ut spolia adepti, procurationes alii et interiorem potentiam, agerent verterent cuncta odio et terrore. corrupti in dominos servi, in patronos liberti; et quibus deerat inimicus per amicos oppressi.   15   20

TACITUS, *HISTORIES* I.ii

pollutus, a, um polluted, defiled
caerimonia, ae, f sacred rite
magna adulteria adultery in high places
infectus, a, um tainted, stained
caedes, is, f slaughter, killing
scopulus, i, m rock
atrocius...saevitum (est) greater cruelty raged
nobilitas, tatis, f high birth
ops, opis, f wealth
omitto, ere, misi, missus refuse
gero, ere, gessi, gestus hold, accept
honos, honoris, m public office
pro crimine were regarded as grounds for accusations
5 *ob + acc.* in return for
exitium, i, n ruin
minus less
praemium, i, n reward

delator, oris, m informer
invisus, a, um hateful
scelus, sceleris, n crime
sacerdotium, i, n priesthood
consulatus, us, m consulship
ut as
spolia, orum, n. pl. spoils, rewards
adipiscor, ipisci, eptus obtain
procuratio, onis, f imperial office
interior, ius: comparative adj. secret, hidden
agerent verterent threw into chaos, created havoc
cunctus, a, um all, every
odium, i, n hatred
in + acc. against
corrumpo, ere, rupi, ruptus bribe, corrupt
20 *desum, deesse + dat.* be lacking
per amicos by their friends

Calgacus' Speech

virtute et genere praestans nomine Calgacus apud contractam multitudinem proelium poscentem in hunc modum locutus fertur:

"quotiens causas belli et necessitatem nostram intueor, magnus mihi animus est hodiernum diem consensumque vestrum initium libertatis toti Britanniae fore; nam et universi coistis et servitutis expertes, et nullae ultra terrae ac ne mare quidem securum inminente nobis classe Romana.

"priores pugnae, quibus adversus Romanos varia fortuna certatum est, spem ac subsidium in nostris manibus habebant, quia nobilissimi totius Britanniae—eoque in ipsis penetralibus siti nec ulla servientium litora aspicientes—oculos quoque a contactu dominationis inviolatos habebamus. nos terrarum ac libertatis extremos recessus ipse ac sinus famae in hunc diem defendit.

"nunc terminus Britanniae patet, atque omne ignotum pro magnifico est. sed nulla iam ultra gens, nihil nisi fluctus ac saxa, et infestiores Romani, quorum superbiam frustra per obsequium ac modestiam effugias. raptores orbis, postquam cuncta vastantibus defuere terrae, iam mare scrutantur. si locuples hostis est, avari, si pauper, ambitiosi, quos non Oriens, non Occidens satiaverit: soli omnium opes atque inopiam pari adfectu concupiscunt. auferre trucidare rapere falsis nominibus imperium, atque ubi solitudinem faciunt, pacem appellant."

TACITUS, *AGRICOLA* 29-30

Calgacus' Speech

Calgacus, a tribal chief from Caledonia (modern Scotland), exhorts his followers before the Battle of Mons Graupius against the Romans, led by Agricola, in A.D. 84. The speech is a dramatic invention by Tacitus.

---

praestans, stantis outstanding
contractus, a, um gathered, collected
proelium, i, n battle
locutus = locutus esse
posco, ere demand
fertur (he) is said
quotiens whenever, as often as
necessitas, tatis, f inevitable situation
5 *intueor, eri* look at, consider
animus, i, m confidence, courage
hodiernum diem: acc. subject of fore this very day
consensus, us, m unity, unanimity
initium, i, n the beginning
fore = futurum esse
universi, ae, a all together
coeo, ire, ii come together, assemble
expers, pertis + gen. free from
ultra beyond us
ne...quidem not even
securus, a, um free from harm, safe
inminente...classe Romana: abl. abs.
inmineo, ere + dat. threaten, hang over
classis, is, f fleet
10 *prior, prius* earlier, former
adversus + acc. against
varia fortuna with varying results
certatum est there was a struggle, there was fighting
subsidium, i, n reserve, help
quia because
eoque and so, and for that reason
in ipsis penetralibus in the most remote regions
situs, a, um situated
servientium: gen. pl. from serviens, ientis of those in slavery
litus, oris, n shore
aspicio, ere look at
contactus, us, m contamination, contact

15 *dominatio, onis, f* tyranny
inviolatus, a, um untouched, undefiled
nos...extremos: acc. object of defendit us, the last peoples (*i.e.*, the most remote) of the world and the last peoples of liberty
recessus, us, m remoteness
sinus famae obscurity
terminus, i, m the end, the limit
pateo, ere lie open
ignotus, a, um unknown
pro magnifico est is regarded as magnificent
20 *fluctus, us, m* wave
saxum, i, n rock
infestus, a, um deadly, hostile
superbia, ae, f arrogance
obsequium, i, n obedience
modestia, ae, f self-restraint, good behaviour
effugio, ere escape, avoid
raptor, oris, m robber, plunderer
orbis, is, m world
cuncta vastantibus: because of their devastation of everything
defuere = defuerunt: desum, esse, fui + dat. fail
scrutor, ari investigate, search
locuples, pletis wealthy
ambitiosus, a, um ambitious, eager for glory
25 *Oriens* the East
Occidens the West
satio, are, avi satisfy
opes, ium, f. pl. wealth
inopia, ae, f poverty
pari adfectu with equal passion, with equal longing
concupisco, ere covet, desire
aufero, ferre plunder
trucido, are murder
rapio, ere steal
imperium = imperium appellant
solitudo, inis, f desert

THE CRITICAL VIEW

Initial Questions

The Disastrous Years
1. What picture does Tacitus give of the state of the Roman Empire at this particular time? Examine carefully which items Tacitus mentions and in what order. To what cause, in your opinion, does Tacitus attribute the disasters?
2. Stylistically, what makes this passage an effective introduction to a period in history? Would this passage be acceptable in a history book today? If not, why not?

Calgacus' Speech
1. Speeches were conventional in Roman historical writing. What purposes might they serve? What does Tacitus reveal by using a direct, albeit invented, speech?
2. Tacitus was interested in revelation and motivation of character. What does this speech reveal of Calgacus' character?
3. Examine Calgacus' final words. To what extent do they sum up the theme of Roman imperialism?

Discussion Questions
1. What do you think Tacitus' purpose was in these two selections?
2. In *Annals* I.1, Tacitus says he writes *sine ira et studio*, without anger or partisanship. Examining the passages of Tacitus here and on pages 36-38, discuss to what extent he achieves his claim.

Further Reading

Caratacus' speech to Claudius on Caratacus' defeat in Britain in A.D. 52 is ostensibly one of submission, yet it conceals a subtle defiance of the Romans: Tacitus, *Annals* XII.35-37.

Tacitus bemoans the liberties lost under Domitian while testifying to the blessings of Trajan's rule: Tacitus, *Agricola* 1-3, 44.

THE VISIONARY VIEW

Tunisian mosaic showing the Roman national poet Vergil between two Muses. The scroll he holds lies open at the beginning lines of the *Aeneid*. (Tunis. Musée du Bardo)

The Return of the Golden Age

Sicelides Musae, paulo maiora canamus!
non omnes arbusta iuvant humilesque myricae;
si canimus silvas, silvae sint consule dignae.

ultima Cumaei venit iam carminis aetas;
magnus ab integro saeclorum nascitur ordo. 5
iam redit et Virgo, redeunt Saturnia regna;
iam nova progenies caelo demittitur alto.
tu modo nascenti puero, quo ferrea primum
desinet ac toto surget gens aurea mundo,
casta fave Lucina: tuus iam regnat Apollo. 10

teque adeo decus hoc aevi, te consule, inibit,
Pollio, et incipient magni procedere menses;
te duce, si qua manent sceleris vestigia nostri,
inrita perpetua solvent formidine terras.

     (continued on page 62)

The Return of the Golden Age

METRE: DACTYLIC HEXAMETRE

In *Eclogue* IV, Vergil predicts the birth of a child whose coming shall see the beginning of a new era, a Golden Age of prosperity and of peace. (From the fourth century on, there was widespread belief among Christians that *Eclogue* IV foretold the birth of Christ.)

Sicelides Musae Sicilian Muses: it was common practice to begin poems with an invocation to the appropriate Muses for inspiration to write; here Vergil invokes the Muses of pastoral poetry
paulo maiora somewhat greater songs
canamus: present subjunctive let us sing
arbustum, i, n tree
iuvo, are please, delight
humilis, e lowly, humble
myrica, ae, f tamarisk: image of the usual unassuming subjects of pastoral poetry
silva, ae, f wood
dignus, a, um + abl. worthy of
ultimus, a, um final
Cumaei carminis of Cumaean song, of Cumaean prophecy: referring to the Sibyl of Cumae, a prophetess of Apollo who lived in the area of the modern Bay of Naples and whose predictions about Rome had filled nine books

5 *ab integro* anew
saeclorum = saeculorum: saeculum, i, n generation; *pl.* ages, centuries
nascor, i am born
ordo, inis, m order, succession
Virgo (i.e., Astraea, Justice)
Saturnia regna the reign of Saturn: referring to an early god of agriculture who reigned in Italy during the former Golden Age; later associated with Cronos, the father of Zeus
progenies, ei, f offspring, race

nascenti puero: dat. after fave
ferrea = gens ferrea the iron age: referring to one of the five ages of humanity—gold, silver, bronze, heroic, and iron—which had been first delineated by the Greek poet, Hesiod, c. 700 B.C. The iron age was the age of troubles and hard work.
desino, ere cease
mundus, i, m universe, world
10 *castus, a, um* chaste, pure
Lucina: another name for Juno as the goddess of childbirth
Apollo: the god of prophecy; as such associated with the Sibylline books and so to be the special god of the predicted new age
adeo even
decus, oris, n distinction, glory
aevum, i, n age
te consule, Pollio: C. Asinius Pollio was consul in 40 B.C. and helped negotiate the treaty between Octavian (Augustus) and Antony which brought peace after years of civil war. Pollio was a patron of poets and introduced Vergil to Octavian
mensis, is, m month
scelus, eris, n guilt, evil deed
vestigium, i, n trace, mark
inritus, a, um useless
solvo, ere free
formido, inis, f dread, terror

ille deum vitam accipiet divisque videbit   15
permixtos heroas, et ipse videbitur illis,
pacatumque reget patriis virtutibus orbem.

hinc, ubi iam firmata virum te fecerit aetas,
cedet et ipse mari vector, nec nautica pinus
mutabit merces: omnis feret omnia tellus.   20
non rastros patietur humus, non vinea falcem;
robustus quoque iam tauris iuga solvet arator;
nec varios discet mentiri lana colores,
ipse sed in pratis aries iam suave rubenti
murice, iam croceo mutabit vellera luto;   25
sponte sua sandyx pascentes vestiet agnos.

"talia saecla," suis dixerunt, "currite," fusis
concordes stabili fatorum numine Parcae.

adgredere o magnos—aderit iam tempus—honores,
cara deum suboles, magnum Iovis incrementum!   30
aspice convexo nutantem pondere mundum,
terrasque tractusque maris caelumque profundum;
aspice, venturo laetantur ut omnia saeclo!

      VERGIL, *ECLOGUES* IV.1-16, 37-52

ille (i.e., the anticipated child)
deum = *deorum*
divus, i, m a god
illis: dat. of agent
pacatus, a, um made peaceful
rego, ere direct, rule, govern
orbis, is, m world
hinc then
firmata aetas strengthened years (i.e., the beginning of manhood)
mari vector the traveller on the sea, the merchantman
nautica pinus ship of pine
muto, are exchange
merx, mercis, f merchandise, goods
tellus, uris, f earth
rastri, orum, m rake, hoe
humus, i, f ground, earth, soil
falx, falcis, f pruning-hook
robustus, a, um strong
taurus, i, m bull
iugum, i, n yoke
arator, oris, m ploughman
disco, ere learn
mentior, iri to counterfeit
lana, ae, f wool
pratum, i, n meadow
aries, ietis, m a ram
suave rubens pleasantly blushing
murex, icis, m purple (dye): referring to the shellfish from which purple dye was obtained
croceus, a, um saffron-coloured, golden, yellow
vellus, eris, n fleece
lutum, i, n dye, a plant used for yellow dye
sponte sua of its own accord, on its own
sandyx, dycis, f vermillion, scarlet
pascens, entis grazing
vestio, ire dress, clothe
agnus, i, m lamb
saecla = *saecula*
fusus, i, m spindle
concors, dis harmonious, of one mind
stabilis, e steady, stable
fatum, i, n fate, destiny
numen, inis, n consent, divine will
Parcae the three Fates: Clotho, Lachesis, and Atropos, who were depicted spinning, measuring, and cutting the thread, or fate, of each human life
carus, a, um dear, cherished
deum = *deorum*
suboles, is, f offspring
incrementum, i, n offspring
convexus, a, um vaulted, arched
nuto, are nod
pondus, eris, n weight
mundus, i, m world
tractus, us, m extent, tract
laetor, ari rejoice

ROME'S MISSION

"excudent alii spirantia mollius aera
(credo equidem), vivos ducent de marmore vultus,
orabunt causas melius, caelique meatus
describent radio et surgentia sidera dicent:
tu regere imperio populos, Romane, memento   5
(hae tibi erunt artes), pacisque imponere morem,
parcere subiectis et debellare superbos."

        VERGIL, *AENEID* VI.847-853

Rome's Mission

METRE: DACTYLIC HEXAMETER

Vergil's *Aeneid* was written to glorify Rome and Augustus. In Book VI of the *Aeneid*, Aeneas, an exile from the fallen Troy, journeys to the Underworld to see the ghost of his dead father Anchises. In the following selection, Anchises assures his son that their descendants, the Romans, have a mission to govern the world.

---

excudo, ere hammer out, fashion
alii other peoples (*i.e.*, the Greeks)
spiro, are breathe
mollius: comparative adv. more gracefully
aes, aeris, n bronze
equidem truly
vivus, a, um living
marmor, oris, n marble
vultus, us, m face
oro, are plead, argue
causa, ae, f court-case
meatus, us, m path, motion
describo, ere map, mark out
radius, i, m rod, compass
sidus, eris, n star, constellation

5 *tu...Romane:* Aeneas as symbol of the Roman people; unlike previous epic heroes, Aeneas deliberately submerges his individual desires and chooses service to the glory and ideal of Rome

rego, regere rule, direct
imperium, i, n authority
memento: imperative of memini remember
tibi: dat. of possession
ars, artis, f skill, art
impono, ere establish
mos, moris, m custom, rule, law
parco, ere + dat. spare
subiectus, a, um the vanquished, the conquered
debello, are crush, subdue, conquer completely
superbus, a, um proud, haughty

THE VISIONARY VIEW

Initial Questions

The Return of the Golden Age
1. Examine the images in the poem carefully and show what each contributes to Vergil's vision of a better time.

Rome's Mission
1. Examine the poetic devices Vergil uses to illustrate the greatness of the achievements of other peoples. Why do you think he developed so carefully the achievements which, he concedes, are not fundamental to Rome's claim to greatness?

Discussion Questions

1. Vergil was an acknowledged supporter of Augustus. How would these selections serve Augustus' program for fostering in the Romans a sense of responsible and disciplined citizenship?
2. Reread the selections from "The Patriotic View" and "The Visionary View." Compare the poetry selections to the prose. What is gained by using verse to express patriotism?

Further Reading

In his national epic, Vergil presents Rome, its history, and its creator-hero, Aeneas, as objects of a divinely ordained destiny to subjugate and civilize the world: Vergil, *Aeneid*, especially *Aeneid* VI.

Rutilius Claudius Namatianus praises the destiny of Rome and its provinces in this selection which begins a poem commemorating Namatianus' return to Gaul after holding an imperial post in Rome: Rutilius Claudius Namatianus, *Poetae Latinae Minores* V.